Michael T Winstanley SDB

Jesus and Young People

Don Bosco
Publications

Don Bosco Publications

Thornleigh House, Sharples Park, Bolton BL1 6PQ
United Kingdom

ISBN 978-1-909080-69-0
©Don Bosco Publications 2020
©Michael T. Winstanley SDB

The moral rights of the author have been asserted

All rights reserved. No part of this publication may be reproduced, stored in a retrieval system or transmitted in any form or by any means without the prior permission in writing of Don Bosco Publications. Enquiries concerning reproduction and requests for permissions should be sent to The Manager, Don Bosco Publications, at the address above.

Front cover illustration *Joy* used with kind permission from David Bowman, artist and owner of David Bowman Art Inc.

Printed in Malta by Melita Press

Dedication

I dedicate this book to the young people I had the privilege of teaching and sharing life with at the Salesian Missionary College, Shrigley Park, (1963–66), Salesian College, Farnborough (1970–72), and the Volunteers I worked and lived with at Savio House (1993–2004, 2010–2013), and also to the young Salesians in formation over many years. They brought me great joy and taught me so much, for which I am deeply grateful.

Foreword

Fr Michael Winstanley has made an outstanding contribution to the mission of the Salesians of Don Bosco for over sixty years as a professed member of the Order. He has assumed significant leadership responsibilities including two terms as Provincial of the Great Britain Province and several terms as Rector of a range of Salesian communities. In the context of this latest book, *Jesus and Young People*, Fr Winstanley's central role in the formation of generations of Salesians and lay people committed to teaching and youth ministry is particularly meaningful in that it explores Jesus' encounters with young people in wide-ranging contexts in the Gospel. It must be emphasised that Fr Winstanley's ministry as a formation guide continues unabated, evidenced by the many invitations he receives both nationally and internationally to share his thoughts on the centrality of the discipleship of Jesus in the life of a Christian.

In his introduction, Michael explains the provenance of the book as a sequel to his *Salesian Gospel Spirituality*, published in July 2020. He suggests that a consideration of the Gospel passages in which young people feature prominently would address a "lacuna", particularly in terms of the Salesian mission which focuses especially on the holistic formation of young people. He refers also to the importance of Pope Francis' Apostolic Exhortation *Christus Vivit* which followed the Synod of Bishops on Young People, Faith and Vocational Discernment in 2018. The latter features at various points within the text and is signposted in the first chapter, *The Daughter of Jairus*, which reminds the reader "we are reminded of our vocation to be sources of life. In every context we are called to discover life, promote aliveness, enable the young (and the not so young) to become more alive in every dimension of their being".

The structure of this twelfth book written by Michael follows that adopted successfully in his previous books with detailed exegesis of specific passages followed by a series of reflections "as an invitation to pondering, prayer and action". He points out from the outset that there are not many stories which describe encounters between Jesus and the young which, perhaps, indicates that this book represents the author's most significant challenge to date. The detailed exegesis does, however, compensate for the paucity of passages, thus observing his maxim of ensuring that the text is accessible to the wide-ranging readership envisioned. At the end of each section of the book there are extensive endnotes which enable the more scholarly reader to engage with greater acuity in the wide range of critical scholarship referenced in this book.

Several themes emerge within the text of this book, and I am confident that others will recognise other emergent themes. First, Michael's emphasis on the primacy of compassion in Jesus' ministry is reflected in several chapters, particularly in Chapters 3 and 8 where the word is referenced eleven and eight times respectively, emphasising the substantial nature of the theme within those passages. Compassion is related particularly to the experiences of young people and the challenges of all engaged in youth ministry to accompany them. The following citation from Chapter Five (*A Father and a Suffering Son*) is especially cogent in this context:

> The story we are considering raises several issues for us to face. How sensitive are we to recognise these situations? Do we experience anything like the father's concern for his son's well-being, or Jesus' compassion for the youth in dire need? Do we summon up our energy and skills and offer our time to respond in an effective way, making real contact with the sufferer.

As one would expect in a book authored by Michael, the concept of relationship features prominently with twelve references in Chapter 11 (*The Prayer of Jesus*) alone. Addressing the issue of the sometimes reluctance of adults to lead young people in prayer is pertinent in a variety of youth ministry settings including school ministry. His suggestion that "part of the problem is our lack of confidence in our ability to help young people in this area. Perhaps the level of our awareness…of God's presence within us, is not buoyant enough to move us to share that relationship with our young people. We cannot reveal to them what we don't have or know personally" is challenging and reflects the iconic statement of the late Cardinal Basil Hume:

> I do not believe that an adult can awaken in a young person a sense of the spiritual if that adult is not at least well on the way to discovering the spiritual dimension of his or her own life. I do not mean that a teacher has necessarily to have found the spiritual meaning to their life, but that spiritual questions must have become real for them. Indeed, in this as in other areas, the best teachers are those who are still learning.[1]

An exaggerated concern for status on the part of some leaders in ecclesial contexts constitutes a third theme. Michael anchors this concern in the context of Jesus approach to leadership which was absolutely counter-cultural to the prevailing environment of his day, citing several key pericope and relating them skilfully to the style of leadership that should be adopted by adults when encountering young people. Among several examples, perhaps the most apposite relates to Jesus' welcoming children following a discussion among the disciples about who was the greatest (Mark 9:33–37). In speaking of "the need to replace attitudes and styles of power, prestige and ambition by humility and generous service", Michael's reflection on this passage is especially germane once again in a wide range of leadership contexts.

I could develop several other themes, for example the focus in the book on the primacy of the Church's mission to the poor in the widest sense. I will, however, allow the reader to dive deeply into the text and discern some further nascent themes. I will conclude by focusing on the audience for the text suggested by Michael, encompassing prayer groups, bible study groups, retreatants, formation communities, teachers, catechists and students at different levels. Based on my experience in the field, I would add to this extensive list those called to leadership positions in Catholic schools. As I read and reflected upon this excellent book, a sacramental vision of leadership emerged from the pages, in essence highlighting that the challenge for all school leaders must, in the first place, be to model their ministry on that of Christ. Inextricably linked to the vocation of the Catholic teacher, Fr Winstanley's comments in relation to the Johannine discourse on the Eucharist that liturgical celebration cannot be divorced from daily living and that we are called and sent to live Eucharist, to be Eucharist are compelling. These words reflect the epochal statement of Pope St Paul VI which represents a fitting conclusion to this foreword since the words encapsulate the writing and the ministry of the author:

---

1   Cardinal Basil Hume, 'The Nature of Spiritual and Moral Development', in Bishops' Conference of England and Wales, *Partners in Mission*, (London: Catholic Education Service, 1997), pp.83–93.

Modern man listens more willingly to witnesses than to teachers, and if he does listen to teachers, it is because they are witnesses. It is therefore primarily by her conduct and by her life that the Church will evangelise the world, in other words, by her living witness of fidelity to the Lord Jesus.[2]

Dr John Lydon KC*HS, SFHEA
Associate Professor of Catholic Education at St Mary's University, Twickenham

---

2   Pope Paul VI, Apostolic Exhortation *Evangelii Nuntianti*, (London: CTS, 1975, n. 41.

Copyright Acknowledgement

Unless otherwise stated, scripture quotations are from:
New Revised Standard Version Bible
Anglicized Edition, copyright © 1989, 1995
National Council of Churches of Christ in the United States of America.
Used by permission. All rights reserved.

Contents

Introduction 1
PART I: Transforming Encounters 7
Chapter One: The Daughter of Jairus 9
    The Story So Far 9
    Two Transforming Encounters with Jesus 11
    Reflections 17
Chapter Two: The Centurion's Son 23
    Reflections 26
Chapter Three: The Son of the Widow of Nain 31
    Reflections 33
Chapter Four: A Gentile Girl 37
    Reflections 41
Chapter Five: A Father and a Suffering Son 47
    Reflections 50
Chapter Six: The Boy with Bread and Fishes 55
    Reflections 59

Chapter Seven: The Markan Children 63
    The First Encounter 63
    The Second Encounter 64
    Reflections 66

Chapter Eight: The Wealthy Young Man 71
    Reflections 73

Chapter Nine: Jerusalem Children 77
    Reflections 81

Chapter Ten: The Markan Ending 85
    Reflections 90

PART II: A Prayer and Parables 97

Chapter Eleven: The Prayer of Jesus 99
    Reflections 101

Chapter Twelve: Dance and Dirge 105
    Reflections 109

Chapter Thirteen: Yes and No 115
    Reflections 117

Chapter Fourteen: Two Lost Sons 121
    The Setting (15:1–2) 121
    The Lost Sons 122
    Departure of The Younger Son 124
    Return and Welcome 125
    The Father and The Older Brother 126
    Reflections 128

Conclusion 137
Bibliography 141

Introduction

Recently I published a book entitled 'Salesian Gospel Spirituality' in which I examined various Gospel themes and passages which, I believe, are central to our way of life and mission as members of the Salesian family. It has occurred to me, however, that I did not seek to reflect on passages in which Jesus encountered young people. Given that our Salesian mission is directed primarily towards young people, this is a significant lacuna, and so I have decided to address this omission. Not long ago the Church sought to recognise more clearly the importance of young people for its own life and mission, and a Synod was held in Rome to consider this. One of the outcomes of that event was Pope Francis' Apostolic Exhortation to the Young, *Christus Vivit, Christ is Alive*. Whilst this document is addressed to all Christian young people, the Pope states that he "is addressing this message to the entire People of God, pastors and faithful alike, since all of us are challenged and urged to reflect both on the young and for the young."[1] I have included some of the Holy Father's thoughts and suggestions in my reflections. It is my hope that this small volume will enable us to meet his challenge.

When we examine the four Gospels, we soon realise that there are not many stories which describe encounters between Jesus and the young. The most famous and significant teenager in the whole New Testament is, of course, Miriam (Mary) of Nazareth, chosen by God to be the mother of Jesus, and so playing a crucial role in the history of salvation.[2] Mark tells of Jesus raising to life the daughter of Jairus, curing the daughter of the Syro-Phoenician woman, and curing the boy with epilepsy. He also refers to Jesus interacting with children on two occasions; Luke and Matthew follow him in this. In Mark a young man escapes during the arrest of Jesus, and an angelic youth appears at the empty tomb. Matthew has a story in which Jesus heals the servant or son of a centurion, and there are versions of this in Luke and John; young people appear in the temple after Jesus has entered Jerusalem. Luke recounts the raising to life of the son of the widow of Nain, and in John's version of the multiplication of loaves and fishes to feed the crowd, it is a young boy who provides the wherewithal for Jesus. All three Synoptists recount an incident where a young man approaches Jesus with a question about how to inherit eternal life. Jesus also provides a few parables in which young people feature: the parable of the two sons, the children in the marketplace, and the two lost sons. He also refers to the young in his prayer.[3]

In all these stories the young people remain anonymous; this is disconcerting, as knowing someone's name is important for us and can make such a difference. Most adults in the Gospels go unnamed as well. Leaving aside the Infancy Narratives of Matthew and Luke, and the passion narratives in all four Gospels, few of the characters who interact with Jesus are named. In Mark, along with the twelve and the two fathers, Zebedee and Alphaeus, we meet John the Baptiser, Levi, Jairus, Herod and Herodias, Bartimaeus and Simon the leper; Mary the mother of Jesus is also mentioned, along with Jesus' four "brothers" (James, Joses, Judas and Simon). Matthew in his narrative omits the names of Jairus and Bartimaeus. In Luke's presentation of the ministry of Jesus, additional names include Simon the Pharisee, and several women who provided for Jesus and the disciples: Mary Magdalene, Joanna, Chuza, who was the wife of Herod's steward, and Susanna. There are also the two sisters Martha and Mary, Zacchaeus, and Cleopas. Johannine additions to the list are Nathaniel, Nicodemus, Lazarus and the high priests Annas and Caiaphas. Most of the people whom Jesus encounters personally during his ministry remain anonymous.[4]

A further issue which confronts us is that, apart from Jairus' daughter, we do not know the age of the young people Jesus encounters or even the small children whom Jesus embraces. The Greek terms used in the Gospels vary, but it is not always clear whether reference is made to children, adolescents or young adults. In that culture girls were married in their early teens, probably including Mary, the mother of Jesus; boys took on responsibility for observing the Law on a par with adults at the age of thirteen, and were usually married by the age of twenty.[5] The rate of infant mortality in Israel at that time was high: about 30% died in infancy and 60% before the age of 16, 70% by their mid-twenties, and 90% by their mid-forties; perhaps 3% reached their sixties.[6] We need to bear this in mind, since nowadays in our quite different culture we use 'young people' terminology as far as the late twenties.[7] It is also important to realise that our attitudes to young people in contemporary Western culture differ from those of the time of Jesus. Joel Green reminds us that children "might be valued for their present or future contribution to family business, but otherwise they possessed little if any intrinsic value as human beings." James Rasseguie notes that children, like slaves, are at the margins of society—dependent, vulnerable waifs. The modern tendency to dote on children is alien to ancient culture.[8] Child labour was a social and economic necessity; youngsters began to work in the fields at the age of six.

It would be a mistake, I believe, to think that the stories listed above record the only occasions in which Jesus encountered young people. As a member of the Nazareth village community he would have met them every day! And as he wandered around the towns and villages of Galilee, engaging with the townsfolk, he would inevitably have also spoken with young people. One feature of the Gospel narratives is often referred to as 'the summary'. For example: "Jesus went about all the cities and villages, teaching in their synagogues, and proclaiming the good news of the kingdom, and curing every disease and every sickness" (Matt 9:35). Very few of these sermons, cures and exorcisms are actually written down. I suspect the same is true of Jesus' encounters with the young. The evangelists have been selective with their sources, and their agendas do not always coincide with our interests. The main concerns of the evangelists are the identity and role of Jesus, and the faith response of the adults involved.

The view of most scripture scholars these days is that Mark was the first to write a Gospel, probably soon after the fall of Jerusalem and the destruction of the temple in 70 CE.[9] He was, in fact, the creator of a new literary genre. For this task he used oral traditions[10] about Jesus which were circulating in the early communities, and probably some written traditions too.[11] This material he arranged in narrative form; the storyline after the Jordan baptism until the concluding Calvary scene depends, not on the historical chronological sequence of Jesus' ministry, but on Mark's own creative design. His aim and emphasis are theological rather than biographical. His story is more like a series of sermons than a string of news bulletins.[12]

There is general, but not universal, consensus that Mark's text was available for Matthew and Luke.[13] They used much of his material but felt free to adapt it to suit their own aims. They also had access to a further document known as 'Q', now no longer extant, which contained many of Jesus' sayings and also some episodes which are not found in Mark. Each seems to have had other sources too. Whilst a few scholars maintain that John had access to their work, most maintain that his Gospel is quite independent.[14] In what follows, when stories are found in all three Synoptists, I have preferred to use Mark's version; for the feeding of the five thousand I follow John.

I shall divide the material into two parts: transforming encounters with Jesus, and words of Jesus (prayer and parables). The format throughout is one which I have frequently used before: an exegetical study of the texts, followed by some personal reflections as an invitation to pondering, prayer and action. There are endnotes for the acknowledgement of sources, the indication of alternative views, points of wider interest, and the possibility of further study. Much of what is contained in the pages which follow, though not all, has already appeared in my other books. I have updated the text when necessary and have here given particular emphasis to the part played by young people. I have tried to write in a non-technical style, hoping that this book will be accessible to a wide readership. As well as for personal study, prayer and reflection, it can also be used by prayer groups, bible study groups, retreatants, formation communities, teachers, catechists, youth ministers, and students at different levels.

In presenting this book I acknowledge my enormous debt to the writings of numerous scholars which I have consulted over the years, which are summarised in these pages, and to which I make frequent reference in the endnotes. Their learning and insights have been instructive and inspirational. I am very grateful to Dr John Lydon, KC*HS, SFHEA, for kindly agreeing to write a foreword to this book, to Ms Annabel Clarkson, for proofreading the text, and Rev Dr Eamonn Mulcahy CSSp., for reading the manuscript and offering an appreciation for the back cover. I thank Fr Bob Gardner, SDB, and Ms Sarah Seddon, of Don Bosco Publications, for their patience, care and expertise in preparing the manuscript for publication.

I dedicate this book to the young people I had the privilege of teaching and sharing life with at the Salesian Missionary College, Shrigley Park, many years ago (1963–66), at the Salesian College, Farnborough (1970–72), and to the volunteers I worked and lived with at Savio House, our Youth Retreat Centre (1993–2004, 2010–2013). They brought me great joy and taught me so much, for which I am deeply grateful. Finally, I thank my Salesian confrères and many other friends, who, over the years, have encouraged and inspired me, especially through their generous and creative dedication to the service of the young. It is my hope and wish that this book may help many readers to come to know more deeply the love of Jesus for the young, and may strengthen them in their generous service.

Michael T. Winstanley, SDB
Thornleigh House, Bolton
October 29, 2020, Feast of Blessed Michael Rua

Endnotes

1   Pope Francis, *Christus Vivit* (London: CTS, 2019), 2.

2   Matthew and Luke tell her story in their infancy narratives. See Michael T Winstanley, *An Advent Journey* (Bolton: Don Bosco Publications, 2014), 101–180; *Walking with Luke* (Bolton: Don Bosco Publications, 2017), 7–64. Pope Francis has a beautiful section on the youthful Mary in *Christus Vivit*, 43–48.

3   Brad H. Young, *Jesus the Jewish Theologian* (Peabody, MA: Hendrickson, 1995), 95, notes that stories about children do not appear in the Dead Sea Scrolls and other writings of the time (pseudepigrapha and apocrypha), or in the writings of Josephus or Philo.

4   In Luke's Infancy Narrative we are introduced to Mary and Joseph, Zechariah and Elizabeth, Simeon and Anna; later we meet Simon the Pharisee and Zacchaeus. In Mark's passion narrative we meet Pilate, Barabbas, Simon from Cyrene, Joseph from Arimathaea, and the women: Mary of Magdalene, Mary the mother of James and of Joses, and Salome.

5   I.Howard Marshall, *The Gospel of Luke* (Exeter: Paternoster Press, 1978), 126, and Christopher F. Evans, *Saint Luke* (London: SCM, 1990), 224, maintain that this took place when a boy was 13. Raymond E. Brown, *An Adult Christ at Christmas* (Collegeville, MN: The Liturgical Press, 1978), 44; *The Birth of the Messiah* (London: Geoffrey Chapman, 1993), 473, maintains that Jesus' visit to Jerusalem at 12 has nothing to do with *bar mitzvah*, which was a much later custom. The general Talmudic principle is that a child reaches manhood at his 13th birthday. *The Jewish Annotated New Testament* (Oxford: Oxford University Press, 2011), (notes on p. 103) states categorically that this is not Jesus' *bar mitzvah*.

6   José A. Pagola, *Jesus, An Historical Approximation* (Miami: Convivium, 2011), 60; James Martin, *Jesus, a Pilgrimage* (New York: HarperCollins, 2014), 77. R. Alan Culpepper, Mark (Macon: Smyth and Helwys, 2007), 179: "Few ordinary people lived out their thirties…much of Jesus' audience would have been younger than he, disease-ridden, and looking at a decade or less of life-expectancy."

7   For the recent Synod the age range for 'young people' was 16–29.

8   Joel B. Green, *The Gospel of Luke,* NICNT (Cambridge: Eerdmans, 1997), 650–651; James L. Rasseguie, *Spiritual Landscape* (Peabody, MA: Hendrikson, 2004), 54; Juan José Bartholomé, *Los Niños en el Ministerio de Jesús de Nazaret*

(Madrid: Editorial CCS, 2018), 10–13. John P. Meier, *Matthew*, (Dublin: Veritas, 1980), 201, describes children as "pieces of property without any rights; powerless to defend themselves, they had to rely totally on others."

9   A long tradition maintains that he wrote in Rome, and a majority of scholars still accept this view. Others suggest a place nearer to Palestine, like southern Syria. Most commentaries on Mark deal with these issues in some detail. See Francis J. Moloney, *Mark: Storyteller, Interpreter, Evangelist* (Peabody, MA: Hendrickson, 2004), 3–18.

10   The literacy level at that time in Israel and the Greco-Roman world was very low. Pagola, *Jesus*, 68, n. 45, states that literacy is estimated at only 10% of the population of the Empire. But people had good memories for the prayers, songs and traditions. See also Whitney Shiner, *Proclaiming the Gospel: First Century Performance of Mark* (London: Continuum, 2003), especially 103–125. For a study of education and literacy at the time of Jesus, see John P. Meier, *A Marginal Jew* (London: Doubleday, 1991), 1:271–285.

11   See Robert K. McIver, *Memory, Jesus and the Synoptic Gospels* (Atlanta: Society of Biblical Literature, 2011), 1: "Before it was written down, the Jesus tradition was almost certainly preserved in human memory for many years." One cannot discount the existence of some written records earlier than the extant gospels. See, James D. G. Dunn, *Jesus Remembered* (Cambridge: Eerdmans, 2002), 173–254.

12   See Morna D. Hooker, *The Message of Mark*, (London: Epworth Press, 1983), 1–4. For an excellent, basic introduction to the Gospels, see Francis J. Moloney, *Reading the New Testament in the Church* (Grand Rapids, MI; Baker Academic, 2015), 113–139.

13   Luke is thought to have written in the mid-eighties CE for a mainly Gentile audience, be that his own urban community or other Church communities in areas of Greece with direct or indirect links to the earlier Pauline mission. Some scholars widen this to the Eastern Mediterranean: Antioch, Caesarea, Ephesus, Corinth and Rome have been suggested. Matthew was written by a third generation Christian, probably in Syria, perhaps Antioch, in the mid-eighties CE.

14   John wrote in the mid to late nineties. The long tradition which identifies three figures: John the son of Zebedee, the Beloved Disciple, and the Gospel's author, is no longer generally held to be accurate. Today some scholars believe that a minor disciple during Jesus' ministry (later known as the Beloved Disciple) had an important role in the founding of the Johannine community and was the source of its tradition about Jesus. This tradition developed through decades of reflection, liturgical celebration, struggles and lived experience, and was eventually fashioned into our Gospel, probably at Ephesus, between 90–100 CE by an unknown but very gifted member of the community, himself a disciple of the Beloved Disciple. Another member of the community (usually referred to as "the redactor") revised the text shortly afterwards, making a few additions. See Raymond E. Brown, *An Introduction to the New Testament* (New York: Doubleday, 1997), 368–371; R. Alan Culpepper, *The Gospel and Letters of John* (Nashville, TN: Abingdon Press, 1998), 29–41.

PART I

Transforming Encounters

CHAPTER ONE

The Daughter of Jairus

In Mark's story of Jesus, the first occasion on which Jesus formally encounters a young person occurs well into the narrative, so it is perhaps useful to be aware of the story so far.

The Story So Far

Mark begins with a clear affirmation of his faith stance, stating unequivocally who he believes Jesus is: "The beginning of the good news of Jesus Christ, the Son of God." Jesus' identity is then proclaimed by God through the words of the prophet Isaiah, as he outlines the role of the forerunner of Jesus, who will be a voice in the wilderness crying out "Prepare the way of the Lord." The Baptist then appears on the scene conducting his ministry: "proclaiming a baptism of repentance for the forgiveness of sins." To avoid misunderstanding about his role and status, John refers to "one more powerful than I" and continues by acknowledging that he is unworthy to stoop down and untie the thong of his sandals. Whereas he himself baptises with water, the coming one will baptise with the Holy Spirit.

Jesus comes from his hometown of Nazareth and submits to John's baptism. As he comes out of the water, the heavens are torn apart and the Spirit descends upon him, and a voice from heaven states "You are my Son, the Beloved; with you I am well pleased." In this way God confirms the identity and mission of Jesus, the anointed one. Immediately he sets about his mission, confronting the powers of evil in the wilderness. Jesus begins his mission as a young adult, in the prime of life.[1]

This section of the Gospel serves as a kind of prologue. The main body of Mark's story begins after John's arrest and imprisonment by Herod. Jesus proclaims the good news: "The time is fulfilled, and the Kingdom of God has come near; repent, and believe in the good news." Jesus then calls his first disciples by the lakeside, Simon and Andrew, who are brothers, and James and John, brothers also. Together they go to the town of Capernaum, which Jesus will make his base, and then attend synagogue. There, Jesus teaches in an authoritative style, and then dramatically expels an unclean spirit. Mark thus introduces the two aspects of Jesus ministry: he preaches and proclaims his message, and he overcomes the power of evil; he proclaims the dawning of God's reigning presence in love, and he makes that presence real. After synagogue he heals Simon's mother-in-law, and later, when the sun has set, marking the end of the Sabbath day, he "cured many who were sick with various diseases and cast out many demons." Next day he leaves Capernaum and begins a tour of the towns throughout Galilee, "proclaiming the message in their synagogues and casting out demons." Approached by a leper, he reaches out to touch him, and with compassion makes him clean.

Mark then introduces a different aspect of Jesus' story, for not everyone is open to his message and his style. Mark brings together a series of five episodes which highlight this opposition. The first and fifth also contain an act of healing, the paralysed man let down through the roof of the house, and the man in the synagogue afflicted with a withered hand. The religious leaders take issue with Jesus' claiming to forgive the sins of the paralysed man, and later with his sharing table with Levi, tax collector now disciple, and his companions, considered to be sinners, on the margins of religious society. Jesus and his disciples are criticised for not fasting, and the disciples for breaking the law by plucking corn on the Sabbath. After Jesus has cured the man with the withered hand during the Sabbath synagogue service, "the Pharisees went out and immediately conspired with the Herodians against him, how to destroy him." From now on Jesus will live and work under the shadow of the cross.

Mark begins the next section of his story with another summary of the activity of Jesus, who is approached by large crowds of people from near and far, seeking healing. Jesus obliges. Then he goes up a mountain and calls his disciples to him, singling out twelve, who are named. They are "to be with him", to share his friendship and life and values, and "to be sent", to share his mission, which is articulated in the familiar terms of preaching and overcoming the power of evil. This is, I believe, a simple but profound understanding of the nature of discipleship for all of us.

A difficult passage follows. First, the family of Jesus seek to restrain him, because people were saying that he was out of his mind. The scribes from Jerusalem come along and accuse him of being possessed by the devil, a charge which Jesus rejects convincingly. Then his mother and brothers come, asking for him. When he is told about this, he turns to those sitting around him and indicates that from now on it is they who are his mother and brothers. A new kind of family is coming into being.

Mark then brings together a number of Jesus' parables, as Jesus gets into a boat and teaches the large crowd with the parable of the sower. The parable of the lamp under a bushel, and two further seed parables follow. Mark stresses that Jesus was wont to preach in this way but indicates that his disciples received clarification in private. After this focus on Jesus as teacher, Mark then brings together a series of episodes in which Jesus performs 'mighty works', notable miracles. The first of these is the incident when Jesus and his disciples set off to cross the lake to the other side and are overtaken by a sudden, severe storm. Jesus is asleep as the disciples panic in fear. They wake him, and he calms the wind and the sea. They disembark on the shore of the country of the Gerasenes, a mainly Gentile territory, and are immediately confronted by a man possessed. Jesus casts out the devils, and they enter a large herd of swine, who career into the sea, to the dismay of their herdsmen. The local people ask Jesus to leave. So, he and the disciples make another crossing, returning to a familiar setting. And it is there that the encounter with a young person, Jairus' daughter, occurs.

Two Transforming Encounters with Jesus

The text reads as follows:[2]

> When Jesus had crossed again in the boat to the other side, a great crowd gathered round him; and he was by the lake. Then one of the leaders of the synagogue named Jairus came and, when he saw him, fell at his feet and begged him repeatedly, 'My little daughter is at the point of death. Come and lay your hands on her, so that she may be made well, and live.' So, he went with him.

> And a large crowd followed him and pressed in on him. Now there was a woman who had been suffering from haemorrhages for twelve years. She had endured much under many physicians and had spent all that she had; and she was no better, but rather grew worse. She had heard about Jesus and

came up behind him in the crowd and touched his cloak, for she said, 'If I but touch his clothes, I will be made well.' Immediately her haemorrhage stopped; and she felt in her body that she was healed of her disease. Immediately aware that power had gone forth from him, Jesus turned about in the crowd and said, 'Who touched my clothes?' And his disciples said to him, 'You see the crowd pressing in on you; how can you say, "Who touched me?" ' He looked all round to see who had done it. But the woman, knowing what had happened to her, came in fear and trembling, fell down before him, and told him the whole truth. He said to her, 'Daughter, your faith has made you well; go in peace, and be healed of your disease.'

While he was still speaking, some people came from the leader's house to say, 'Your daughter is dead. Why trouble the teacher any further?' But overhearing what they said, Jesus said to the leader of the synagogue, 'Do not fear, only believe.' He allowed no one to follow him except Peter, James, and John, the brother of James. When they came to the house of the leader of the synagogue, he saw a commotion, people weeping and wailing loudly. When he had entered, he said to them, 'Why do you make a commotion and weep? The child is not dead but sleeping.' And they laughed at him. Then he put them all outside, and took the child's father and mother and those who were with him, and went in where the child was. He took her by the hand and said to her, 'Talitha cum', which means, 'Little girl, get up!' And immediately the girl got up and began to walk about (she was twelve years of age). At this they were overcome with amazement. He strictly ordered them that no one should know this, and told them to give her something to eat. (5:21–43)

As is evident from the text, there are two encounters here. Jesus raises to life the daughter of a synagogue leader named Jairus, and he heals a woman suffering from a long-term haemorrhage problem. These two episodes belong together, for they are linked structurally by the Markan literary device of framing or sandwiching, whereby one story is used as an interlude within the other, allowing the first part to develop.[3] The delaying tactic heightens the tension of the drama. Both stories are concerned with the themes of faith and life. Each can be understood and interpreted in the light of the other. "The flavour of the outer story adds zest to the inner one; the taste of the inner one is meant in turn to permeate the outer."[4] A young woman and an older woman benefit from the kindness and power of Jesus, and are given life. The interwoven story is perhaps Mark's masterpiece in terms of narrative art.[5] Although my main focus lies with Jairus' daughter, in order to do justice to Mark's skilful storytelling, we need to consider both episodes together.

Back in home territory after his foray into a Gentile region, where the people wanted him to leave, Jesus is immediately confronted on the western shore of the lake with a large crowd of more positively disposed people. The president of the local synagogue approaches him. The exact structure of synagogue governance varied from place to place, depending on the size of the village or town.⁶ The official is not a rabbi or scribe; his role probably entails presiding over the conduct of synagogue worship, arranging the services, assigning readers, appointing preachers, preserving order, maintaining the building and managing the finances. Mark sees him as a high-standing member of the local Jewish establishment, and, after identifying his office, provides his name, Jairus.⁷ In a manner hardly appropriate for one of his standing, but which betrays the depth of his distress, he casts aside his dignity and throws himself at Jesus' feet, his desperate concern and faith wordlessly expressed in his bodily posture. All else has failed. He then puts his genuine belief in Jesus' healing power, authority and closeness to God into words, as he repeatedly pleads: "My little daughter is at death's door. I beg you to come and lay your hands on her so that her life may be saved." The wording is significant; the term used in the Greek for daughter (*thygatrion*) indicates affection as well as age or size. Jairus asks Jesus to lay hands on her. This was normal in contemporary descriptions of healing, and also a frequent feature of Jesus' own healing ministry. The text speaks of the child's being "saved" (rescued from the power of death) and "living". This language can be interpreted at two levels, and a Christian reader would sense a deeper level of meaning, namely, being saved and experiencing eternal life.⁸ Jesus cannot but respond to Jairus' request. Without saying a word, he immediately sets off through the thronging, jostling crowd, accompanying Jairus to his home.

As they walk along, Jesus is approached by a woman who has been suffering from haemorrhages for twelve years, a sensitive, private concern of chronic menstrual bleeding. This is the only Gospel story dealing with gynaecological problems. The contrast between the woman and Jairus is striking.⁹ She seems to have done the rounds of the medical profession to no avail, and this has drained her financial resources. Perhaps originally, she was a woman of some means, who is now becoming severely impoverished.¹⁰ It is clear that her situation is quite hopeless and is even deteriorating; death is looming; there is nowhere else to turn. Her distress is compounded by the fact that her ailment was considered to render her constantly ritually unclean, and liable to communicate this to anyone with whom she has contact. Thus, she is an outcast from society, unable to play an active role in the community of Israel.¹¹ In contrast with Jairus, she is outside the chosen people of God, a rejected one. Because of her condition she may have been divorced or dismissed by her husband.¹²

Having heard about Jesus' reputation, she comes up through the crowd from behind, probably because of her ritual uncleanness rather than from shyness or modesty. Breaching the purity barrier, with courage she approaches Jesus and touches his cloak, convinced that this would suffice for a cure.[13] In doing so, given her condition and the blood taboo, she runs the risk of considerable disapproval, exposing a holy man to ritual uncleanness. It was unusual for a woman to plead her own cause. She obviously has faith in Jesus, faith of a kind, faith that he can make a difference, faith tinged perhaps with a little superstition. She believes that because he is a holy man, his healing power can freely flow at a mere touch, without him being aware of it.[14] Such views were not uncommon at the time; clothing was considered an extension of personality. She is proved right and is cured, delivered from her torment, feeling the transformation, on the spot.[15]

She is not, however, allowed to melt back into the crowd. One of the aspects of this incident which appeals to me very strongly is the way in which Jesus moves from anonymity to personal encounter. Jesus is aware that someone has touched him, and that "power had gone out of him." He can distinguish between healing touch and ordinary touch. He knows that God has acted through him.[16] Jesus openly asks who has touched him. His question is greeted rather disrespectfully and insensitively by the disciples, who are locked into common sense, and consider his question absurd, given the press of the crowd. Jesus ignores them and persists in his attempt to meet the woman personally, looking around at the crowd.

The woman is filled with awe and reverential fear because of what has happened to her. "Fear and trembling" means holy awe; she recognises that she has been touched by the power and presence of the Kingdom.[17] She comes forward, falls at his feet, as Jairus had done, and "told him the whole truth." Jesus can now relate to her personally, and he speaks to her with great warmth, respect and affection: "My daughter, your faith has restored you to health; go in peace and be free of your complaint." His words confirm her cure and affirm what she has done. She is addressed as "daughter", and brought back into the chosen people of God, and into the new family of the Kingdom.[18] A relationship is established. Her faith is acknowledged; it was sufficient to enable her to take the risk involved in reaching out to him. Her first coming to Jesus brought healing, her second coming the assurance of salvation.[19] Jesus' words deflect somewhat the magical tone of the story by stressing her faith as the source of healing. The Greek word is again "save", implying that along with the physical and social cure, and her restoration to normal life, comes the offer, the gift of salvation. "Peace", a standard biblical dismissal, is more than freedom from embarrassment and anxiety. It connotes the wholeness and completeness of life which derives from being drawn into relationship with the Lord.[20] "Be free" is better translated as "remain healed", "continue to be well", since for this woman, in returning to normal life, a new life is beginning. The sensitive beauty of the story masks the offence which Jesus' contact with her would have caused others.

While Jesus is speaking with the woman, the focus switches back to Jairus and his daughter. Having successfully pleaded with Jesus that he accompany him the short distance to his home, Jairus is suddenly confronted with a message that his daughter has in fact died, with the rider that there is no point in troubling the Master further. It is now too late for him to do anything. All hope has been lost. Common sense must prevail. Jesus overhears the news. The Greek verb (*parakouein*) can mean both overhear and ignore. Jesus certainly overhears but does not ignore what has been communicated; rather, he encourages Jairus to do so. For he urges and invites him: "Do not be afraid; keep on believing." An even greater degree of faith than that shown previously is now demanded. Despite all the odds and the pressure, Jairus summons up the faith to respond. Along with the girl's parents, Jesus allows only Peter, James and John to accompany him, as will later be the case at the Transfiguration, on the Mount of Olives, and in Gethsemane.[21] The three seem to form an inner circle, and are "with" Jesus at episodes in Mark's story where significant revelation is involved.

On their reaching the house, Jesus observes the commotion, the unrestrained weeping of the people there, probably the official professional mourners along with members of the household. There were well-established rituals for beginning the grieving process, which made it possible for family members to give vent to their feelings without restraint or embarrassment.[22] Jesus enters the house and asks what all the fuss is about, for "the child is not dead but asleep."[23] Jesus is taking a well-known euphemism and twisting it. The difference between death and sleep is its permanence. Jesus is not using the euphemism as a pointer to eschatological hope and last day resurrection. Although he has not yet seen the young woman, Jesus knows that he is about to raise her from the permanence of death immediately. So "death is declared mere sleep not because of a cagey medical diagnosis or a comforting euphemism or a general eschatological hope, but because Jesus wills in this particular case to make death as impermanent as sleep by raising the girl to life."[24]

The onlookers, aware that the child is well and truly dead, burst into laughter. This is the only miracle story in the Gospels where Jesus is made the direct object of such scornful ridicule. He personally excludes the crowd to avoid a public spectacle. His forceful physical action is also unique in the Gospel miracle stories.[25] Jesus then takes Jairus, his wife and his three disciples into the room in which the girl is lying. They are present as witnesses, not helpers.[26] Without a prayer or special technique, but with great tenderness, Jesus takes her by the hand,[27] and calls her back to life: *Talitha kum!* which is translated as "Young lady, I tell you to arise." *Talitha*, indicating smallness and youth, also has affectionate overtones.[28] Aramaic words are used in only two miracle stories in Mark.[29] Aramaic was the original language of the tradition, and of Jesus, and its retention shows their importance.

At Jesus' word, the child arises at once and begins to walk around, her activity confirming what has happened. Jesus has raised her to life, and he restores her to her mother and father and family life, later suggesting that she be given something to eat—a deeply human touch (perhaps her parents are frozen with astonishment), but also an indication that she is real and not a ghost. The reader is now informed of her age; she is twelve years old. The reaction of the parents is described in unusually graphic language,[30] indicating that they are utterly astounded, ecstatic, which is hardly surprising, given the exceptional nature of what has occurred! Jesus then gives them strict orders not to let anyone know about it. This seems rather odd in the circumstances, as neighbours and parents know that she was dead; it is an injunction impossible to fulfil. Jesus' point is that the emphasis should not be on the wonderful, but on the power and authority of God present in his word. Also, such actions, taken in conjunction with his proclamation of the Kingdom, would pose a threat both to Herod and the religious leadership. It is to his death and resurrection, through which he responds to God's saving design, that the commands to silence point forward.[31]

The reader notes Jesus' use of the term "arise", in addition to "save" and "live". For early Christians "sleep" was a euphemism for death but indicated a death from which the believer would be raised. The child's restoration to life is a symbol of Christian resurrection.[32] For those who have faith, Jesus can transform death into life and salvation. Salvation and faith are major themes in both stories. Jairus and the woman show amazing faith in the midst of unbelief and common sense.

I mentioned earlier that the stories of the raising of Jairus' daughter and the cure of the woman with the haemorrhage are linked or paired. Besides the strong faith theme, one element which is common is the detail that the child is twelve years old, and the woman's affliction has been troubling her for twelve years, debarring her medically and socially from childbearing.[33] Whilst some believe this is coincidental,[34] others do not: "The girl of twelve years of age—now marriageable—gets up and walks. She rises to womanhood. The young woman, who now begins to pour forth her life in menstruation, and the older woman who experiences menstruation as a pathological condition, are both restored. They are 'given' new life."[35] The older woman was probably prevented by her medical condition and social state from the possibility of having a child.³⁶ Now both are rescued from death and rendered capable of birthing new life. They can "go and live in Shalom, in the well-being and happiness of God's reigning presence, which has touched their lives in Jesus of Nazareth."³⁷

One element of Jesus' compassion is his reaching out to touch, an element which would have shocked the religious elite. Earlier he has touched the physically and religiously unclean leper, and he takes the hand of Simon's mother-in-law; later, at a meal in Bethany during the final week of his life, he allows himself to be anointed by another woman. He is touched here by the woman with vaginal bleeding; in fact, the word "touch" occurs three times in the episode and is clearly a key concept. He takes the hand of Jairus' daughter and raises her from her bed; she is dead (and so unclean), and is also of marriageable age, and so the gesture could be understood as ambiguous. It was unheard of for a respected rabbi to take a woman's hand or touch her or be touched by her, especially in public, and the gesture was open to misinterpretation. Jesus shows remarkable freedom, as he breaks through cultural, social and religious barriers and ritual taboos to be close to those in need. In both miracles Jesus is in contact with the unclean; his touch brings healing, wholeness and life.³⁸

Reflections

Jairus, an anxious father, approaches Jesus. In his concern and need, he ignores issues of status, and places his trust in the power and kindness of Jesus. His faith is subsequently put to a severe test, when news is brought that his daughter has died. He responds to Jesus' recommendation to continue believing and experiences the joy of seeing her restored to life and to the family. The faith of the woman in the story takes a different path, as she wrestles with her affliction and with the social and religious stigma attached to it. There is determination and conviction about her, as in her hopelessness and trust, she takes the risk of touching Jesus, and is brought to wholeness. Both Jairus and the unnamed woman are presented to us as models of faith. In both cases their faith stands in contrast with the common-sense approach to life, as witnessed in the responses of the disciples, Jairus' servants and the mourning party. In our increasingly secularised and sceptical world, faith is so frequently viewed as odd and quite ridiculous. Living by faith remains a challenge.

Two aspects of the person of Jesus are brought out in these stories, besides his remarkable healing power, which overcomes evil and introduces the Reign of God. First, he relates to people so sensitively and appropriately. His initial response to Jairus' request is positive and immediate. Without hesitation he sets off with him to his home to bring healing to his daughter. Aware that someone has been healed through contact with him, he seeks to establish a relationship. There is compassion in the way he addresses the woman, and warmth, as he acknowledges her faith, and welcomes her into new life. Despite the ridicule of the locals, he reassures the dead girl's parents by his confidence and determination, as he accompanies them into the house. Again, there is warmth and affection in his manner and voice as he raises the girl to life and restores her to them, even suggesting, doubtless with a smile, that they should give her something to eat. Secondly, there is a stunning freedom about him as he disregards convention and religious taboos. He is not concerned with public opinion, nor put off by the disparaging comment of his disciples, nor the ridicule of the crowd. His attention is focused on people in need; his priority is to enable them to experience the presence of the Reign of his loving and compassionate Father.

Although passive till the end of the whole sequence, the daughter of Jairus is really the unknowing catalyst. Young people, especially when in need, can do just that. We cannot but respond to them. This is true at all kinds of levels, from the simple everyday to the more demanding and dramatic. Even when the relationship is not warm and deep, as was not the case with Jairus, it is difficult for us human beings to remain inactive and unresponsive. As Jesus in this encounter raises the young woman into her teens, gives her new life, with all its exciting and challenging possibilities, we are reminded of our vocation to be sources of life. In every context we are called to discover life, promote aliveness, enable the young (and the not so young) to become more alive in every dimension of their being. Both she and the older woman are rendered capable of bringing new life into the world. They are reminders of this wonderful gift and responsibility which we share.

An interesting feature of both stories is the element of touch; the verb is used many times. Jesus is initially requested to lay his hands upon Jairus' daughter; he is touched by the woman, and he takes the girl by the hand. The touch of Jesus is healing and life-giving. Such touching would be a source of shock and displeasure for the religious elite. Touch is such an important human faculty; it is a language, a two-way means of communication. But it can be an ambiguous language. For young and old there is safe touch, the focus of which is the need of the other person, rather than one's own needs. It is can be an expression of warmth, love, care; it brings comfort, support, communion and, as in these stories, it can bring healing, forgiveness, wholeness, life. In recent years we have become much more sensitive to issues around touch because of safeguarding. For touch can cause hurt, discomfort, harm; it can be an expression of selfishness, power and evil. Whilst acknowledging the need to be sensitive and the danger of being misunderstood, it cannot be right for people, especially the young, to be starved of warm, nurturing touch. This is an also important field for education; young people need to know how to say "stop" when touch is hurtful to them.

Mark uses the child's experience of death being transformed into life as a pointer to the later experience of Jesus himself. The vocabulary used is a clear indication of this. And his experience sets the scene for us, his followers. Because of Jesus, for us death is not the end but the beginning. This whole Markan sequence exudes hope, meaning and a sense of future.

Endnotes

1   Pope Francis, *Christus Vivit,* 23.

2   For Luke (8:40–56), she is the only daughter. Matthew provides a much-abbreviated form in 9:18–26 and omits the name of the girl's father.

3   Many commentators believe that the two stories originally existed separately, and that Mark or a pre-Markan tradition joined them together. For other examples of this literary technique see 3:19–35; 5:21–43; 6:6b–29; 11:12–25; 14:1–11; 14:53–72, and also 1:4–8; 1:21–28; 4:3–20: 6:7–30; 13:5–27; 14:18–25. Other terms to describe the technique, which is not a Markan invention, are insertion, intercalation, interpolation, dovetailing, interweaving, heterodiegetic analepsis: see M. Eugene Boring, *Mark. A Commentary*, (NTL Louisville & London: Westminster John Knox, 2006), 157; Meier, *A Marginal Jew*, 2:708.

4   N. Tom Wright, *Mark for Everyone* (London: SPCK, 2001), 58; Wilfrid Harrington, *Mark* (Dublin: Veritas, 1979), 70. Hugh Anderson, *The Gospel of Mark* (London: Oliphants, 1976), 151, notes that the two complement each other in meaning.

5   Brendan Byrne, *A Costly Freedom* (Collegeville, MN: Liturgical Press, 2008), 99.

6   Meier, *A Marginal Jew,* 2:845, n. 30; Culpepper, *Mark,* 171. Large cities would have more officials and greater functional differentiation.

7   For Elizabeth S. Malbon, *In the Company of Jesus: Characters in Mark's Gospel* (Louisville: Westminster John Knox, 2000), 157–159, Jairus is one of three Jewish religious leaders who is presented positively. He is the first religious leader to show interest in Jesus. Boring, *Mark,* 158, notes that he is probably wealthy, for his daughter has a separate room; ordinary peasants had only one room in the house(also Culpepper, *Mark,* 178; George Martin, *The Gospel according to Mark* (Chicago: Loyola, 2005), 122).

8   Dennis E. Nineham, *St. Mark* (London: Penguin Books, 1963), 160; Harrington, *Mark,* 72, 75–76; Morna D. Hooker, *The Gospel according to St. Mark* (London: A&C Black, 1991), 148; Anderson, *Mark,* 152; Martin, *Mark,* 115; Culpepper, *Mark,* 172. Boring, *Mark,* 157, notes that in the biblical world to be sick was already to be in the grasp of death, and to be healed was to be restored to life. Resurrection imagery is present.

9   Boring, *Mark,* 157–158, notes the contrasts: Jairus is named, male, wealthy, a leader of the synagogue, a parent concerned about his sick daughter; he approaches Jesus publicly, seeking healing for her, and receives a greater miracle privately, and is commanded to tell no one. The woman is nameless, poor, excluded from the synagogue; she has no children and can have none; is concerned about the living death she bears in her own body; she approaches Jesus surreptitiously, receives the miracle in intimate secrecy, but is compelled by Jesus to make it public. Both come to Jesus with faith derived from hearing about him from others; their faith leads both to overcome the impurity barrier; both respond with fear and amazement rather than gratitude. Jesus' salvific power is extended to both. Both cases reflect the newness of the Christian community generated by the Christ event.

10   Boring, *Mark,* 159; John R. Donahue, and Daniel H. Harrington, *The Gospel of Mark.* Sacra Pagina 2. (Collegeville, MN: Liturgical Press, 2002), 174, point out that in antiquity only those with financial means visited physicians.

11   Lev 15: 25–30. See Francis J. Moloney, *The Gospel of Mark. A Commentary*, (Peabody, MA: Hendrickson, 2002), 107; Hooker, *Mark,* 148; Martin, *Mark,* 116. Boring, *Mark,* 159, notes that the issue is the power associated with blood that must be safeguarded.

12   Donahue & Harrington, *Mark,* 180. Martin, *Mark,* 116, points out that according to Lev 20:18, sexual intercourse was forbidden. She was unable to enter the Temple and would be unwelcome in the synagogue.

13   "Touched" is the main verb, after seven participles. The Greek style in this second story is rather different. Others seek to touch the cloak of Jesus in 3:10; 6:56. Meier, *A Marginal Jew,* 2:709, thinks the popular religious ideas smack of magic.

14   Culpepper, *Mark,* 174, observes that the imperfect tense of the verb "saying" (v. 28) implies that she was repeating this to herself over and over again.

15   Elizabeth S. Malbon, *Mark's Jesus. Characterisation as Narrative Christology*, (Wac: Baylor University Press, 2009), 84, considers that she makes a "bold move of gaining access to the power of the in-breaking rule of God that is available through Jesus, and it is successful."

16   Hooker, *Mark,* 149: in the LXX *dynamis* is used primarily for God's power. Donahue & Harrington, *Mark.* 175, link this with 1:7 and 1:10, Jesus as the "stronger one", the Spirit-endowed prophet. Nineham, *Mark,* 161, prefers the translation: "the power proceeding from him (i.e. his messianic power of healing) had gone forth."

17   Moloney, *Mark,* 108: see 1 Cor 2:3; 2 Cor 7:15; Phil 2:12; Eph 6:5. Donahue & Harrington, *Mark,* 175, refer to human fragility in the presence of divine power. She is not "afraid" because she has been found out. Byrne, *A Costly Freedom,* 101, takes this as a Christological confession.

18   Martin, *Mark,* 119, suggests that "daughter" is both a term of affection and a proclamation that there is a bond between them; she is no longer cut off from human relationships.

19   Denis McBride, *The Gospel of Mark* (Dublin: Dominican Publications, 1996), 91. Donahue & Harrington, *Mark,* 176, note the link between faith and salvation; saving faith describes the confidence and boldness whereby people surmount obstacles to come to Jesus (2:5; 9:23; 10:52).

20   Anderson, *Mark,* 154; Culpepper, *Mark,* 176; Eduard Schweizer, *The Good News according to Mark* (London: SPCK, 1971), 118.

21   9:2; 13:3; 14:33. Andrew joins them in 13:1.

22   Wright, *Mark,* 62. For details of mourning practices, see Donahue & Harrington, *Mark,* 177; Culpepper, *Mark,* 177. For Boring, *Mark,* 162, given that the dead were often buried on the day they died, the funeral has already begun.

23   The word "child" (*paidion*) has a nuance of affection (Donahue & Harrington, *Mark,* 177). For sleep as a euphemism for death, see Matt 27:52; 1 Cor 11:30; 15:16; 1 Thess 4:11.

24   Meier, *A Marginal Jew,* 2:844, n. 26c.

25   Meier, *A Marginal Jew,* 2:787; 850, n. 60.

26   In the Old Testament Elijah and Elisha go alone (1 Kings 17: 19, 23; 2 Kings 4:33, 36–37), as does Peter in Acts 9:40.

27   Donahue & Harrington, *Mark,* 177, note that corpse impurity was the most severe of all impurities, so by touching the girl he is violating cultural codes.

28   *Talitha* is affectionate for 'little lamb'. The "young lady" of the Greek translation (*korasion,* diminutive of *korē*) can be used for a girl approaching marriageable age. *Koum* or *kum* is the common word for "get up". Matthew and Luke omit the Aramaic phrase.

29   Here and 7:34, the story of the deaf-mute. The Greek verb (*egeirein*) for "arise" is used for the resurrection of Jesus in 14:28; 16:6; the verb for "got up" (*anistēmi*) is likewise used of Jesus in 8:31; 9:9, 31; 10:34. "The density of language about death and resurrection here is evidence that the Markan readers are to see this narrative as a foreshadowing of Jesus' resurrection and of their own awakening from the sleep of death." (Donahue & Harrington, *Mark,* 178).

30   Repeated in 16:8.

31   Moloney, *Mark,* 111. For Byrne, *A Costly Freedom,* 103, the meaning of the raising can only be grasped by those who are being schooled in belief in Jesus' own resurrection, which is never to be separated from his death. Boring, *Mark,* 163, also emphasises the links with Jesus' resurrection.

32   Hooker, *Mark,* 148. Donahue & Harrington, *Mark,* 181, comment: "The raising of Jairus' daughter is for Mark's readers the prototype of their own hope that their God is a God not of the dead but of the living (12:27)."

33   Hooker, *Mark,* 147–150.

34   Meier, *A Marginal Jew,* 2:756, thinks that it may have been a factor which

brought the stories together originally.

35   Moloney, *Mark*, 111.

36   Hooker, *Mark*, 150. Boring, *Mark*, 158, lists the contrasts and parallels between the two: "both are female; both are unclean and cannot be touched; both are restored to community, family and sexuality; both are given life, but also become life-givers: the healed woman can now bear children, the young woman now stands on the threshold of puberty, marriage and family; both are called "daughter"; both can now be mothers. They are both affected by a time span of twelve years: the one entered her living death the year the other was physically born. On the same day, when everything seemed hopeless, each is delivered into new life. The verb *sōzō* is used of both, and both are saved from more than physical sickness and death. One has the bold faith that dares to touch; the other is absolutely passive and unable to do anything for herself but receives Jesus' life-giving touch." See also Culpepper, *Mark*, 171.

37   Elizabeth S. Fiorenza, *In Memory of Her* (New York: Crossroad, 1983), 122–124; see Donahue & Harrington, *Mark*, 181; Byrne, *A Costly Freedom*, 102.

38   Moloney, *Mark*, 111; Byrne, *A Costly Freedom*, 103. Pope Francis, in *Christus Vivit*, 1, writes: "everything he touches becomes young, new, full of life."

CHAPTER TWO

The Centurion's Son

The next Gospel episode featuring a young person which I wish to consider is found in Matthew's story of Jesus. It takes place in Capernaum quite early in Jesus' ministry soon after he has delivered the Sermon on the Mount. A centurion approaches Jesus, seeking help for his sick son. There is a parallel version in Luke in which the centurion sends some of the village elders to intercede with Jesus, and then some of his friends, rather than approach him personally. There is a similar story in John, which occurs in Cana, in which a royal official asks Jesus to come to heal his son, who was on the point of death.[1]

Matthew's Gospel opens in a different way from that of Mark. He introduces Jesus as the Messiah, Son of Abraham, Son of David, and continues with what is usually termed an Infancy Narrative. In this he offers a genealogy of Jesus, commencing with Abraham. This is followed by the story of Jesus' birth, the visit of the Magi, the flight of the family into Egypt, thus avoiding Herod's massacre of infants, and their return to settle in Nazareth. We are all familiar with these stories, which we hear and celebrate in Advent and Christmastide. After the arrival of John the Baptiser on the Judean scene, Jesus goes to be baptised, and then moves into the desert, where he is tempted. After this the ministry begins with the call of the first disciples, and then a journey throughout Galilee in which Jesus teaches, heals and exorcises, attracting great crowds from Galilee, the Decapolis, Jerusalem and beyond the Jordan. This is followed by the Sermon on the Mount, three chapters devoted to the teaching of Jesus.

At this point Matthew picks up the Markan narrative, but thoroughly reorders and streamlines his material, also inserting two episodes not included there. After his ministry of the word in the great sermon, Jesus, the messianic teacher, now exercises a messianic ministry of healing. In both words and works, Jesus shows great authority. There are nine miracle stories, grouped in threes. The encounter between Jesus and the centurion is located in the first group between the cure of the leper and the healing of Simon's mother-in-law (and others); all three individuals were disadvantaged in different ways in the Jewish community. The section concludes with a quotation from Isaiah (53:4): "He took our infirmities and bore our diseases." This suggests that Matthew sees him as the Servant. Given that in the Infancy Narrative, when the scribes, in replying to Herod's enquiry as to the place of the birth of the Messiah, quote the scriptural text which refers to "a ruler who is to shepherd my people Israel", I believe that Jesus is exercising his shepherding role in reaching out to others in this way.[2]

The text, which is both a miracle narrative and pronouncement story, reads as follows:

> When he entered Capernaum, a centurion came to him, appealing to him and saying, 'Lord, my servant is lying at home paralysed, in terrible distress.' And he said to him, 'I will come and cure him.' The centurion answered, 'Lord, I am not worthy to have you come under my roof; but only speak the word, and my servant will be healed. For I also am a man under authority, with soldiers under me; and I say to one, "Go", and he goes, and to another, "Come", and he comes, and to my slave, "Do this", and the slave does it.' When Jesus heard him, he was amazed and said to those who followed him, 'Truly I tell you, in no one in Israel have I found such faith. I tell you, many will come from east and west and will eat with Abraham and Isaac and Jacob in the kingdom of heaven, while the heirs of the kingdom will be thrown into the outer darkness, where there will be weeping and gnashing of teeth.' And to the centurion Jesus said, 'Go; let it be done for you according to your faith.' And the servant was healed in that hour. (8:5–13)

The setting is the frontier town of Capernaum, which Jesus seems to have made his base. On arriving back there, Jesus is met by a centurion from the military garrison manned by soldiers in the service of Herod Antipas.[3] He probably hails from Syria and is a Gentile. Aware of Jesus' reputation, and addressing Jesus respectfully as "Lord", he outlines his problem and concern, explaining that his son is lying paralysed at home in considerable distress.[4] His illness, though not mortal, as in Luke, clearly precludes the possibility of his bringing him to Jesus.

The response of Jesus to this approach can be taken in two ways. Usually, it is understood as a statement: "I will come and cure him." Jesus responds immediately, even expressing his willingness to come to the centurion's house in order to bring the boy healing and relief. He is prepared to have dealings with a Gentile and even enter his home, thus incurring ritual uncleanness and some local displeasure. The centurion is clearly dismayed by this unexpected offer which exceeds his original request, and, again addressing Jesus as "Lord", acknowledges his unworthiness to welcome him under his roof. He recognises the authority of Jesus, which comes from God, going on to voice his conviction that a word of Jesus, without making the short journey, will be sufficient to effect a cure. For, in his position and with his army experience, he knows what authority is all about, and is well acquainted with the power of a word of command. If he can command with a word, all the more so can Jesus. His trust in the efficacy of Jesus' word is amazing.

An alternative view understands Jesus' words as a question, constituting an initial hesitation or rebuff, as in the later episode of the Canaanite woman (15:21-28). In effect, surprised at the request, Jesus is asking "Am I supposed to come and heal him?"—and this in a Gentile house, thus breaking the rules on purity. Scholars who are of this mind maintain that such reluctance is consistent with Jesus' later response to the Canaanite woman. The centurion is aware of his unworthiness; he is not expecting a personal visit to his house; he is conversant with Jewish rules about ritual cleanness; he respects Jesus' authority, which renders such a visit unnecessary; he offers Jesus an alternative course of action.[5]

On hearing this reply, Jesus is amazed, the only occasion when Matthew uses this term of Jesus,[6] and he observes to those with him that he has not found insight and faith of such quality amongst the people of Israel to whom he has directed his mission. The man has shown some awareness of Jesus' closeness to God. He has also sensed that as a Gentile he is not entirely excluded from Jesus' care. Jesus then authoritatively makes a telling statement.[7] Looking ahead into the future, and echoing the vision of the prophets of old, Jesus claims that there will be many Gentiles, people from east and west, who will come to share the messianic banquet of the heavenly Kingdom with the great patriarchs Abraham, Isaac and Jacob, whilst their true natural heirs will be cast out.[8] The centurion, like the earlier Magi of the Infancy Narrative, is the forerunner of these.

In the opening verse of his Gospel, Matthew has presented Jesus as Son of Abraham. Abraham is the father of the Jewish people, but also the one in whom all the nations of the world would be blessed (Gen 12:3). In 4:15, as

Jesus inaugurates his ministry, making his home by the lake in Capernaum, Isaiah's reference to "Galilee of the nations" is recalled (Isa 8:23–9:1). Later in the narrative Matthew quotes Isaiah concerning the Spirit-filled Servant who will "proclaim justice to the Gentiles...And in his name the Gentiles will hope" (12:15–21; Isa 42:1–4). In his final discourse Jesus predicts the preaching of the Gospel to all the nations (24:14). Finally, the focusing of his ministry on the Jews, "the lost sheep of the house of Israel", as expressed in his dialogue with the Canaanite woman, is superseded after his death and resurrection (15:24; 10:5–6). For, back in Galilee the risen Lord gathers his disciples, scattered by the striking down of the sheep. He makes to them his final statement: "All authority in heaven and on earth has been given to me. Go therefore and make disciples of all nations..." (28:18–19). With the dawning of the new age, the blessings of the Kingdom are made available to all.

Jesus' words concerning the future also constitute a severe warning or threat for his Jewish hearers, who are in danger of missing the opportunity to embrace their destiny. A warning is also sounded for Matthew's church in a different and later context; the community must not be complacent or exclusive; they must continue vigorously to believe.[9]

The story proper concludes with Jesus telling the centurion to return home with the assurance that, in accordance with his faith, his request will be granted. In fact, his son is healed, and healed at a distance. The power or authority of Jesus' word is evident; but the emphasis in the story is probably more on the centurion's remarkable faith, his trust in Jesus, than on the miracle. "Although Jesus has come only for the lost sheep of Israel, the restriction is overcome when he meets genuine belief. Faith conquers the separation between Jew and Gentile."[10] Perhaps the healing at a distance is intended to reflect the restriction of Jesus' ministry to Israel; maybe it is a spatial metaphor symbolising the historical fact that Gentile participation in the blessings of the Gospel is separated in time from the earthly ministry of Jesus.[11]

Reflections

Following the traditional interpretation of the story, Jesus is clearly presented as a man of authority. He is probably surprised at being approached for a cure by a Gentile, a Gentile of some standing. Unusual as this is, and contrary to the normal thrust of his ministry, he responds immediately with great openness, even volunteering to go to the centurion's home in order to cure his son. Clearly, such a visit was not part of the petitioner's scenario. Jesus is prepared to incur ritual defilement in order to meet the youngster and effect the healing, and he is also open to incur criticism and hostility from the townsfolk for his trouble. There is a remarkable freedom and openness about him. He publicly expresses his amazement at the man's extraordinary faith. Adopting the other interpretation of the story, Jesus manifests his flexibility, his openness to change his attitude when faced with strong faith. He generously acknowledges in public the faith he has encountered.

It is the centurion's remarkable faith which stands out from the narrative. He clearly believes in the power of Jesus to heal his son; he trusts that his Gentile background will not prove an insurmountable obstacle. He is aware of his poverty and emptiness. He shows humility in readily acknowledging his unworthiness to have Jesus under his roof. For him, a word from Jesus is enough.

In commenting so favourably on the Gentile's faith, Jesus puts him forward as an exemplar. This is the case not only for the Jews of the town in which the encounter took place; it is true for us today. There is something engaging and attractive about the man's humble awareness that he has no rights and cannot demand a cure for his son. Such poverty of spirit must be a characteristic which we share when we approach Jesus in our need. The man's words have been included in the new form of our eucharistic celebration. They sum up the dispositions which are appropriate for our welcoming of the Lord into the home of our hearts.

The centurion's son is said to be paralysed, and is a Gentile, beyond the faith contours of Israel. And yet Jesus is prepared to go to see him at home, and also to liberate him from his crippling illness, opening up for him the possibility of an ordinary life alongside his peers. The fact that there is no face-to-face encounter does not detract from the compassionate openness and generosity of Jesus. Jesus' attitude and behaviour invites us to be free, creative and courageous in our efforts to bring healing and liberation to the young people we encounter, and also to young people far away.[12] Like Jesus, we need to be willing to move beyond our comfort zone and reach out to young people who may be difficult, disengaged, awkward, isolated. We may need to overcome preconceptions and prejudices, our own and those of others, and be prepared to incur criticism, suspicion and even hostility in our attempts to reach out and assist. The centurion, in his love for his son and desire for his healing, goes to Jesus and requests his help. Jesus is the only one who can do anything for him. This is a reminder to us when faced with similar, difficult situations. We need to take to Jesus in prayer those for whom we are concerned and for whom we seek healing. In our prayer we entrust the sufferer to Jesus' compassion. We need to be people who trust in his power and loving care.

Endnotes

1   Matt 8:5-13; Luke 7:1-10; John 4:46-54. I have reflected on Luke's version in *Walking with Luke*, 241-244, and on John's presentation in *Symbols and Spirituality* (Bolton: Don Bosco Publications, 2007), 98-99. The story is not found in the Gospel of Mark.

2   See my *Salesian Gospel Spirituality* (Bolton: Don Bosco Publications, 2020), 156-159.

3   Meier, *A Marginal Jew*, 2:721, notes that most centurions were ordinary soldiers who progressed through the ranks; the number of troops they commanded varied; it could be 30 or 60 men, not necessarily 100. They exercised more than simply military duties, including building and diplomatic roles; they were not a homogeneous group. Herod Antipas had a private army, probably mainly Gentiles, and adopted Roman military nomenclature. Donald A. Hagner, *Matthew*. Word Biblical Commentary. 2 vols. (Nashville: Nelson, 2000), 1:203, entertains the possibility that he was a Roman. Francis W. Beare, *The Gospel according to Matthew* (Oxford: Blackwell, 1981), 207, suggests that for Herod the purpose was to keep the restless native population of northern Galilee under control. Daniel Harrington, *The Gospel of Matthew*. Sacra Pagina 1. (Collegeville, MN: Liturgical, 1991), 113, raises the possibility that the man could be retired.

4   "Lord" is polite and respectful; for Christian readers it would have greater significance. Matthew's Greek (*pais*) is ambiguous, perhaps reflecting earlier Aramaic ambiguity, and can mean servant or son; the Evangelist does not resolve the ambiguity; in either case we are dealing with a young person. The NRSV opts for servant, as do many commentators. The versions of Luke (*doulos*), a servant, and John (*huios*), a son, reflect different interpretations; Luke also refers to him later in the story as a boy (*pais*). I have followed Ulrich Luz, *Matthew*. 3 vols. (Minneapolis, MN: Augsburg Fortress, 2001, 2005, 2007), 2:10, n. 17, and Hagner, *Matthew*, 1:204, in preferring "son"; the latter, *Matthew*, 1:204, notes that the deep concern of the centurion is more natural in the case of a son. H. Benedict Green, *The Gospel according to Matthew* (Oxford: Oxford University Press, 1975), 99, maintains that there is no obstacle in Matthew's account to taking the sick boy as the centurion's son; also David Hill, *The Gospel of Matthew* (London: Oliphants, 1978), 158. In Luke and John, the problem is that the servant or son is near to death; in Luke with some unspecified illness; in John with a fever; in Matthew he is painfully paralysed, but not in danger of death.

5   Stephen Voorwinde, *Jesus' Emotions in the Gospels* (London: T&T Clark, 2011), 18-19; Harrington, *Matthew*, 113, takes this view; also William D. Davies and Dale C. Allison, *A Critical and Exegetical Commentary on the Gospel according to Saint Matthew* (London: T&T Clark, 2004), 120; Luz, *Matthew*, 2:10. Donald Senior. *Matthew* (Nashville: Abingdon Press, 1998), 98, follows most commentators in opting for the traditional opinion; also Eduard Schweizer, *The Good News according to Matthew* (London: SPCK, 1976), 213; Hagner, *Matthew*, 1:204. Beare, *Matthew*, 207, believes the view is over-subtle; in Matthew Jesus usually takes the initiative and sets his own course. Robert H. Gundry, *Matthew* (Grand Rapids, MI: Eerdmans,

1994), 143, rejects the indignant question idea; also, Hill, *Matthew*, 158. Meier, *Matthew*, 83–84; in *A Marginal Jew*, 2:719, n. 182, he outlines in detail the issues involved, but concludes by disagreeing with the alternative view, and preferring the traditional declaration opinion. One strong reason is Jesus' immediate response to the marginalised leper in the previous incident, infringing the Law and ritual rules in the process; also, the centurion is not bargaining for an alternative, but is waiving the favour offered. The idea of Jesus going to the house was not part of the original request, and so cannot be a cause of indignation. Hagner, *Matthew*, 1:204, notes that the "my" roof is emphatic, which expresses the centurion's sensitivity to Jewish mores.

6   Also, Mark 6:6; both here and in Mark, Jesus' amazement is a response to the presence or absence of faith. Usually the verb (*thaumazein*) applies to other people: the disciples in Matt 8:27; 21:20; the crowds in 9:33; 15:31; the Pharisees in 22:22; Pilate 27:14. Matthew rarely refers to Jesus' emotions. Faith is an important theme for Matthew, which he frequently highlights (e.g. 9:2, 22, 29; 15:28; 17:20; 21:21; 23:23).

7   Meier, *Matthew*, 84 and Senior, *Matthew*, 99, maintain that Matthew has added these verses from 'Q' to the original healing story. Luke places them in a different context (13:28–29). The apocalyptic imagery of "outer darkness, weeping, and gnashing of teeth" are typical Matthaean judgement metaphors. See also Davies & Allison, *Matthew*, 121; Hagner, *Matthew*, 1:206.

8   Isa 25:6–8; 49:12; Mal 1:11. Hagner, *Matthew*, 1:205–206, notes that the prophets' view was that the banquet would be a Jewish affair, with Gentiles receiving an overflow. The coming of many referred to the return of the diaspora Jews (from Egypt and Babylon) to Israel. Now it is the Gentiles who are being called; the "heirs of the kingdom" will in large part be rejected. The true sons of the kingdom are those who respond positively to Jesus. (See 21:33–44; 22:1–10); Luz, *Matthew*, 2:9.

9   Meier, *Matthew*, 84; Schweizer, *Matthew*, 215–216.

10   Davies & Allison, *Matthew*, 121.

11   Beare, *Matthew*, 209.

12   In *Christus Vivit*, 74, Pope Francis refers to young people who suffer forms of marginalisation and social exclusion for religious, ethnic or economic reasons. He lists those who are pregnant, the scourge of abortion, the spread of HIV, various forms of addiction (drugs, gambling, pornography), street children, and observes that these situations are doubly painful and difficult for women.

Chapter Three

The Son of the Widow of Nain

Early in the Gospel of Luke there is an episode, not found elsewhere, in which Jesus raises a young man to life. So far in Luke's story of Jesus, after the Infancy Narrative and the baptism and temptations of Jesus, Jesus begins his ministry by visiting his hometown of Nazareth. In the synagogue he is invited to read, and chooses a passage from Isaiah which serves as his mission statement, outlining the way he will exercise his ministry by bringing good news to the poor, release to captives, sight to the blind, freedom to the oppressed, and proclaiming the jubilee year. His townsfolk initially respond positively, but the mood changes; they take umbrage at his words and seek to kill him, but he escapes and goes to Capernaum. Luke then follows Mark's outline, with some modifications: in the synagogue Jesus preaches and performs an exorcism, he heals Simon's mother-in-law and others who come thronging to him for help. He calls his first disciples, heals the leper and the paralysed man, calls Levi to discipleship, copes with challenges about fasting and Sabbath observance, and heals a man with a withered hand. He then chooses the twelve. There follows the Sermon on the Plain, his briefer form of Matthew's Sermon on the Mount. After this, Luke recounts the episode of the centurion's servant in Capernaum, before transporting his readers to Nain, where the focus is a widow who has lost her son. Neither of these episodes is found in Mark. The text reads:

> Soon afterwards he went to a town called Nain, and his disciples and a large crowd went with him. ¹²As he approached the gate of the town, a man who had died was being carried out. He was his mother's only son, and she was a widow; and with her was a large crowd from the town. ¹³When the Lord

saw her, he had compassion for her and said to her, 'Do not weep.' ¹⁴Then he came forward and touched the bier, and the bearers stood still. And he said, 'Young man, I say to you, rise!' ¹⁵The dead man sat up and began to speak, and Jesus gave him to his mother. ¹⁶Fear seized all of them; and they glorified God, saying, 'A great prophet has risen among us!' and 'God has looked favourably on his people!' ¹⁷This word about him spread throughout Judea and all the surrounding country. (7:11-17)

Nain, which is not mentioned elsewhere in the Bible, was a small town some six miles from Nazareth and five from Capernaum, where Jesus had just healed the centurion's servant, who was seriously ill.[1] Jesus goes to the town accompanied by his entourage and a large crowd. As they approach the town gate, they meet a funeral procession moving out to the place of interment, probably a cave on the hillside. It was the custom for burials to take place outside town and as soon as possible after death. Our attention is focused throughout on the sad plight of the woman: she has lost her husband and is therefore a widow, and now her only son, the support and hope of her life, has also died. She is alone, without economic support or social status, and very vulnerable. A life of hardship, loneliness and poverty beckons.[2] The woman is accompanied by a large crowd of mourners, for it was considered meritorious to attend funerals and share in the grieving. Besides, a death in a small town touches everyone. Mourning was greater for an only child. The professional mourners would also be noisily present.

No request is made of Jesus to intervene; the initiative is entirely his. Jesus, described here as "the Lord",[3] is deeply concerned, and in this tragic situation is "moved to compassion" for the woman. The technical verb for compassion (*splanchnizesthai*) is used here. First, he tells her that she need weep no more. In showing such care in public for the woman, Jesus once again crosses the boundaries of religious propriety and custom.[4] He then ignores the risk of incurring ritual defilement by approaching and touching the bier on which the corpse lay in a linen shroud (Num 19:11). The bearers halt, and Jesus, speaking to the corpse with a word clearly audible to the crowd, raises the youth to life again: "Young man, I say to you, get up!"[5] The youth sits up and begins to speak again. Then, showing his deep concern for the woman, Jesus "gave him back to his mother." Jesus' action in restoring life to the deceased young man is clearly remarkable, but it is subsumed into his care for the grieving mother.[6] Jesus restores life to her, too, and reconstitutes the family. In the story there is no mention of the woman's faith, nor that of the onlookers. The focus is entirely on Jesus' compassion, on liberating mercy freely bestowed.

The witnesses to what has occurred are numerous. Their initial reaction is one of fear and awe. Jesus has done what only God can do. Then they burst into praise of God, chorus-like, recognising that "a great prophet has arisen among us", and concluding with words which closely echo the words of Zechariah's *Benedictus:* "God has shown his care for his people."[7] The compassion of Jesus, his deep concern for human suffering, reveals the presence amongst them of God's saving mercy.

Reflections

The woman in this story has no active role. She represents the many bereaved and vulnerable in our world, people whose lives are in shreds, whose futures look grim. The loss of a child is always extremely difficult to bear, whether the child is young or old. In her emptiness and loss, she can only receive. Her inner poverty, however, is a catalyst. Her need moves Jesus to compassion, a compassion which transforms her life and that of her son. And yet she is a valuable reminder to us of our own inner poverty, our poverty of being. Awareness of our poverty, our areas of inadequacy and need, can open us to the healing and life-giving presence of Jesus. It is when we find ourselves in situations of loss that we can be found by him, loss of health (of sight, hearing, mobility), loss of independence, loss of friends and family, loss of position or job, loss of confidence. In our lives, there are many death experiences which we have to embrace and work through. Jesus comes as the compassionate one who will be supportively with us, sustaining us in our struggle. He can also open up new possibilities, transforming death into life.[8]

Concerning Jesus, Denis McBride observes that Jesus is the one who takes the initiative, who speaks first, who notices suffering and desolation, and who does not bypass them along the road. He is not afraid of getting his hands dirty, of being regarded as unclean, in his movement of compassion. When he meets suffering at the crossroads, he does not take the route of least resistance and flee from the face of pain. He transforms it by his touch and by his word.[9] As his disciples, we are called to follow his way.

I wonder how the young man felt, waking up on a bier and surrounded by lots of noisily mourning people and a distraught mother. He must have wondered what was going on! His first reaction was to speak, to seek to communicate. Perhaps when he reached home with his mother and friends, and heard the whole story, he would have realised the loving concern of Jesus from Nazareth and shared the wonder of the crowd and the gratitude of his mother. He could now embrace his life again, the life which lay ahead of him, with all its challenges and possibilities. And, family life reconstituted, he was able to resume his responsibility of caring and providing for his mother.

There are many young people in our world and country today who shoulder the responsibility of caring for a parent, and sometimes also for their siblings.[10] Because of natural pride, and also fear of possible implications, they can be reluctant to reveal this, even though it can be interfering with their education, health and well-being. We need to be sensitive, to pick up the signals, to find ways of reaching out without frightening them, ways of giving them hope and support, transforming their lives. In supporting them, we will also be helping their families. Like Jesus, we need to be compassionate people, willing to touch the bier and get involved, and in that expression of compassion be creative.

The young man of Nain, raised to life by Jesus, was in a position to help and support his mother as she grew older and feeble, less able to cope with life's demands. The culture of Jesus was the culture of the extended family, and of respect for the elderly. There are many scriptural references which highlight this: for example, "Listen to the father who begot you, and do not despise your mother when she is old" (Prov 23:22).[11] The fourth commandment reflects this fundamental attitude and way of living. Perhaps this prompts us to ponder the situation of elderly people in our world and culture today, and the way in which we seek to respond to their needs, physical, emotional and spiritual.

In *Christus Vivit*, 187–201, Pope Francis addresses the issue of the relationship between young and old. He stresses the danger of a rupture between the generations, and the positive effects of intergenerational relationships. "When young and old alike are open to the Holy Spirit, they make a wonderful combination" (see Ps 148:12–13; Joel 3:1). "If we journey together, young and old, we can be firmly rooted in the present, and from here, revisit the past and look to the future. To revisit the past in order to learn from history and heal old wounds that at times still trouble us. To look to the future in order to nourish our enthusiasm, cause dreams to emerge, awaken prophecies and enable hope to blossom. Together, we can learn from one another, warm hearts, inspire minds with the light of the Gospel, and lend new strength to our hands."[12]

Endnotes

1   The two incidents are carefully paired by Luke; they also illustrate his penchant for juxtaposing episodes with a female and male protagonist. Although found only in Luke, the story about the widow of Nain is not a Lukan creation, but is derived from his special source material, which he has edited. Meier, *A Marginal Jew,* 2:797, notes that the anchoring of the story in the obscure Galilean town of Nain, now shown by archaeology to have had a gate, as well as the presence of some possible Semitisms in the text, argues for the origin of the story among Jewish Christians in Palestine. With some hesitation, he inclines to the view that the story goes back to some incident involving Jesus at Nain during his public ministry. Bartholomé, *Los Niños,* 44, n.43, suggests that it is no coincidence that Nain is not far from Shunem, where Elisha raises a boy to life (2 Kings 4:18–37).

2   Also, Joseph A. Fitzmyer, *The Gospel according to Luke.* 2 vols. (New York: Doubleday, 1981, 1985), 1:658; Luke T. Johnson, *The Gospel of Luke,* Sacra Pagina 3. (Collegeville, MN: Liturgical Press, 1991), 118; Evans, *Luke,* 346; John T. Carroll, *Luke: A Commentary* (Louisville: Westminster John Knox Press, 2012), 165. Care for widows is a prominent theme in the Old Testament (Deut 10:18; 14: 28–29; 24:17–21; 27:19; Job 24:3; Ps 146:9; Isa 10:1–2).

3   "Lord" is used of Jesus after his resurrection, but Luke anticipates this usage during the ministry.

4   Francis J. Moloney, *This is the Gospel of the Lord (C)* (Homebush: St Paul Publications, 1991), 134.

5   The Greek is *neaniske,* the Latin *adolescens;* hence the translation "young man".

6   Brendan Byrne, *The Hospitality of God* (Collegeville, MN: Liturgical Press, 2000), 70; Green, *Luke,* 290, observes that here the healing is the restoration of the woman within her community.

7   1:68; in 1:78 *splanchna* is used. The Greek verb is best translated as "visited", a term which is used in the Old Testament to describe God's saving interventions on behalf of his people (Gen 21:1; Exod 4:31; Ps 105:4).

8   Pope Francis, *Christus Vivit,* 20, writes: "If you have lost your inner vitality, your dreams, your enthusiasm, your optimism and your generosity, Jesus stands before you as once he stood before the dead son of the widow, and with all the power of his resurrection he urges you: 'I say to you, arise!'"

9   Denis McBride, *The Gospel of Luke* (Dublin: Dominican Publications, 1991), 96.

10   Pope Francis, *Christus Vivit,* 262, observes that sometimes young people "must take on responsibilities that are not proportioned to their age and that force them to become adults before their time."

11   Proverbs 20:29 states: "The glory of young men is their strength, but the beauty of old men is their grey hair." Personally, I find this encouraging!!

12   *Christus Vivit,* 199.

CHAPTER FOUR

A Gentile Girl

Our next story concerns a woman of Syro-Phoenician origin,[1] whose daughter is possessed by an unclean spirit, and who approaches Jesus seeking a cure for her. The episode is found in both Matthew and Mark. We shall follow the latter's version. After raising Jairus' daughter to life, Jesus returned to his native Nazareth, but his townsfolk rejected him. He then sent out his disciples on mission; before their return, Mark recounts the death of the Baptist. The sequence of events which follows in the overall Markan narrative consists of five episodes. It begins with the feeding of the 5000, followed by a lake crossing. There follows a controversy between Jesus and his opponents about cleanliness and the old traditions. Finally, there are the two stories of the Syro-Phoenician woman, in which there is a reference to bread, and the healing of a deaf mute. These two stories in Mark's mind belong together and are clearly and explicitly placed in a geographical setting which is Gentile territory.[2] This overall structure is then immediately paralleled in the subsequent literary block containing five episodes. This time, 4000 are fed; there is a brief lake crossing, a controversy (the demand for a sign), a reference to loaves of bread, and a healing, this time of a blind man.[3] Mark's structure is carefully and cleverly crafted. Theologically, it is particularly significant for the evangelist that the miracles occur on behalf of Gentiles. Mark is keen to illustrate how Jesus sets about breaking down the traditional barrier which separates Jew and Gentile.[4]

The text of our story reads:

> From there he set out and went away to the region of Tyre. He entered a house and did not want anyone to know he was there. Yet he could not escape notice, but a woman whose little daughter had an unclean spirit immediately heard about him, and she came and bowed down at his feet. Now the woman was a Gentile, of Syrophoenician origin. She begged him to cast the demon out of her daughter. He said to her, 'Let the children be fed first, for it is not fair to take the children's food and throw it to the dogs.' But she answered him, 'Sir, even the dogs under the table eat the children's crumbs.' Then he said to her, 'For saying that, you may go—the demon has left your daughter.' So, she went home, found the child lying on the bed, and the demon gone. (7:24–30)

The last place explicitly referred to in Mark's narrative was Gennesaret, where Jesus and the disciples moored the boat after crossing the lake subsequent to the feeding of the multitude. Then, "wherever he went, into villages or cities or farms, they laid the sick in the marketplaces, and begged him that they might touch even the fringe of his cloak; and all who touched it were healed." After recounting the discussion with the religious leaders concerning the traditions about ritual washing before meals, and Jesus' further explanations to the crowd and then to the disciples, the evangelist indicates a change of scene, for from there Jesus moves away from Israel and "set out and went away to the region of Tyre."[5] This is clearly Gentile territory, though there were many Jewish inhabitants there too. Tyre was an ancient Phoenician cosmopolitan city, mentioned in the Old Testament, situated about forty miles from Capernaum.[6] It still flourished as an important urban seaport, and its territory bordered on Upper Galilee. The inhabitants were not friendly towards the Jewish minority; they were an economically dominant and oppressive group.[7] No explanation for the journey is provided, and it is not stated that the disciples accompanied him.[8] Possibly Jesus wanted to leave Galilee because it was under Herod's jurisdiction, or maybe this was just another way of getting away from the Jewish crowd.[9]

Jesus enters a house, a typically Markan feature.[10] Clearly, he is seeking some privacy. However, his presence cannot go unnoticed; anonymity is difficult to come by. A local woman gets to hear that he is in the vicinity and searches him out.[11] She enters the house and falls respectfully at his feet as a suppliant.[12] The verb used (*prospiptein*) means to place oneself at the mercy of another. Her reason for approaching Jesus is her concern for her daughter,[13] who has an unclean spirit. She trusts his ability to remedy her condition. The narrator points out unequivocally the theologically crucial fact that, being of Syro-Phoenician origin, the woman is a Gentile; her culture is Greek. As the first

Gentile to make such a request in Mark, she introduces an air of suspense into the narrative's unfolding.[14]

The woman begs Jesus to cast the demon out of her daughter. Her pleading is an expression of her motherly concern for her daughter and an admission of the hopelessness of her situation. It is also an expression of her trust in his power and his willingness to help her. The response of Jesus is surprising and something of a puzzle: "Let the children be fed first; for it is not fair to take the children's bread and throw it to the dogs." Jesus' words seem rather harsh, shocking, insulting even, a put-down, and at odds with what would be expected after the previous controversy, and with Jesus' normal mode of acting.[15] His reply clearly suggests that he understands his mission as confined to the people of Israel, who saw themselves as God's privileged sons and daughters. His vocation is not to spread the Gospel to the Gentile world, but to tell the Jewish people that their long-awaited deliverance is at hand. "First" suggests that when this is accomplished it would be time for the Gentiles. For the moment it is important that he does not lose his primary focus.[16] Despite the difficulties which have arisen in his ministry, the negativity experienced, Israel remains the privileged recipient of his gift of bread. However, Israel has in fact been fed in the lakeside banquet, and the amount of leftovers was considerable.

Dogs were considered to be unclean scavengers, and were usually regarded negatively by the Jews, unlike people of Greek culture, who kept dogs as pets. The term 'dog' was a common traditional Jewish term of contempt for Gentiles. Some view the exchange as teasing banter,[17] or consider the diminutive form, puppy or little housedog, as humorous or as softening the harshness. Some understand the saying as parabolic: Jesus draws a picture of a home scene in which children take priority over the dogs.[18] Others understand the words of Jesus as a challenge to the woman to justify her request. The gospel of the Kingdom has not been proclaimed to the Gentiles. Jesus' miracles are closely linked with his preaching, since they are a sign and an expression of the breaking in of the Kingdom and can occur only where there is faith. The woman's request seems to fall outside this context; she is perhaps taking advantage of the opportunity provided by the presence of the miracle-worker.[19]

The woman is undeterred, and replies: "Sir, even the dogs under the table eat the children's scraps." Children and dogs can eat at the same time. "Sir" is the normal polite form of Gentile address; it is not used elsewhere in Mark in this way; it implies a recognition of his authority.[20] Probably Mark sees a deeper significance in it here, as it also means *Lord*, and expresses insight into his identity.[21] The woman seems to take no offence; she accepts what Jesus says; she accepts the analogy and its implications, acknowledging that Israel has priority in God's saving plan. She, like the household pets of her culture,[22] is content to feed on the crumbs from the Jewish table. She recognises that she has no rights, no claims to assistance; that she cannot merit a cure, is utterly empty-handed, totally dependent; but she still trusts that he will do what she asks. It is not only a question of persistence fuelled by her need and her deep concern for her daughter. Nor is it simply that her womanly intuition senses from the look in his eyes or the tone of his voice that he is a man of immense compassion. Her reply, adapting Jesus' metaphor to her own need, also indicates some glimmering of understanding concerning the Kingdom, the recognition "that the children are already being fed, and that, in spite of their recognised priority, there is hope for her now."[23] She is convinced that it is from Jesus, the Jewish Messiah, that salvation is to be obtained.[24] She moves into a context of faith, perceiving the presence of God's power in Jesus. This he recognises, doubtless along with the exquisite quality of her repartee, and grants her request, assuring her that when she reaches home again, she will find her daughter restored. The miracle is worked at a distance, which is unusual in the case of an exorcism. "For saying that, you may go; the demon has left your daughter." Though the woman's faith is not explicitly mentioned, the cure is linked to the same kind of faith response which is characteristic of the other miracles described earlier in the narrative.[25] The healing power of the Kingdom is available for Gentiles too.[26]

The woman takes Jesus at his word and returns to her home, where she finds her daughter lying on her bed, liberated from her affliction. She is a woman of remarkable faith. The concluding expression of wonder, which is a typical element in stories of healing, is not found here, perhaps because she went home alone.[27] In the overall context, her faith stands in stark contrast to the legalism and self-righteousness of the Jewish religious leaders, which is illustrated in the section of the Gospel leading up to this incident, a section in which Jesus has challenged and upturned some fundamental Jewish tenets.

In this story Jesus has reached out to a Gentile. But it would be inexact to speak of a programmatic mission of Jesus to the Gentiles as a body. This incident, along with a few others, are a departure from Jesus' plans, intentions and normal practice. They are exceptions and special cases, and something of an anomaly. They are, however, intimations of what will come later.[28] In keeping with Jewish tradition, Jesus thought of God as choosing Israel. Like the prophets before him, he understood his mission as directed to Israel. It would be for the renewed and obedient Israel to undertake the mission to the nations.[29] This is the wider perspective envisaged for the Servant by Isaiah.[30] The distinction between Jew and Gentile and their relative places in the order of salvation remain in force. There is, however, a refreshing freedom and flexibility about

Jesus. Rigidity is foreign to his make-up. The woman's response to the presence of Jesus foreshadows the future offer of salvation to the Gentiles, and their coming to faith in him.[31] Perhaps the fact that the cure has been performed at a distance is to be understood as symbolic of the salvation which comes to the Gentiles, hitherto far away.[32]

Reflections

One significant factor of the story is the crossing of boundaries. Jesus crosses into fairly hostile Gentile territory. The woman crosses the religious and gender barriers, and the social barrier between itinerant preacher and landed property owner. She crosses the divide between stereotypical male dominance and female submissiveness, between woman and unknown male in a private place. "Jesus' harsh reply would be expected in a first-century androcentric culture; what would be shocking are the courageous reply of the woman and Jesus' ultimate capitulation."[33]

This woman comes to Jesus as a mother pleading for the healing of her daughter. Like Jairus earlier in Mark's narrative, she is desperate. Her maternal love and concern are obvious, leading her to disregard accepted boundaries and an initial rejection. Her persistence is striking, as are her perception and her quick-witted repartee. Fundamentally, as Jesus finally acknowledges, she is a woman of remarkable faith. She reminds us of a typical mother's love for her child, devotion to their well-being. So often do mothers go to enormous lengths to protect, bring healing and wholeness to their children. Such love, I believe, is a revelation of God's parental love for us.[34]

Jesus has gone to Tyre seeking privacy. He is located, and his plan is thwarted. Initially, he seems reluctant to accede to the woman's importunate request. In the end he changes his mind. His fundamental openness and flexibility win through. He is uncomfortable with rigidity and fixed boundaries. The person who benefits most from Jesus' presence in the region of Tyre is the woman's daughter, a Gentile like her mother. She is set free from the evil holding her bound. A new life beckons her, and perhaps a deeper appreciation of her mother's love and care. But again, Jesus reaches out beyond his comfort zone to bring healing and wholeness to this young Gentile, and to include her in the blessings of the Kingdom. That is always his desire for young people. The child in the story can do nothing for herself. She is fortunate in having such a good mother. There are, however, many young people in difficulties of various forms who have no one to care and no one as an advocate. Here there is a need for friends, pastors, teachers to become involved on their behalf.[35] In the past many religious communities have been founded precisely for this and have done wonderful work. This work continues with ever increasing lay involvement. In today's world the needs are no less urgent.

The story gives us a glimpse of the struggle which took place in the early Church in coming to terms with the inclusion of Gentiles, first in the Christian community, and then at the eucharistic table, a struggle with which Mark and his community were not unfamiliar. The woman articulates the Gentile perspective in this divisive area.[36] Mark's readers would see this episode as the tip of the iceberg and as the initial penetration of Jewish exclusivism, the crumbling of the barrier of separation.[37] Barriers are transcended and must continue to be transcended. "If Jesus yielded to the cry of faith while the division between Jew and Gentile still stood, how much more should the Christian Church go out to the Gentiles."[38]

In our Church today there are perhaps boundaries of a different kind which need to be transcended. The initial reluctance of Jesus was later reversed. This should be a cause for optimism, an invitation to persistence, and a challenge to abandon any trace of rigidity. His example directs us towards openness, and the overcoming of prejudice and preconceptions. There are people in our country and in our Church who are prejudiced against the young, quick to blame, criticise and even condemn. This can occur in the treatment of ethnic minorities too. This is not the way of Jesus. We need to be aware of our own personal tendencies and seek to change them, when necessary, so that we share the mind and heart of Jesus. We are called to be advocates of the young in his name.

Endnotes

1 A Phoenician from Syria, rather than from Libya in N. Africa.

2 In 7:24 and 31 the indications are explicit. The two stories probably existed separately in the earlier tradition; see Moloney, *Mark,* 144; Meier, *A Marginal Jew,* 2:660. Malbon, *Company,* 52, comments that perhaps Luke was not the only evangelist to establish male-female pairings.

3 Feeding (6:35–44 and 8:1–9); lake crossing (6:45–52 and 8:10); controversy (7:1–23 and 8:11–13); reference to bread (7:24–30 and 8:14–21); a healing (7:31–37 and 8:22–26).

4 Boring, *Mark,* 206, reminds us of the two levels of the story: a woman seeking healing for her daughter, and the problems of Mark's church, now

predominantly Gentile. Jewish and Christian integration, especially in the celebration of the eucharist, was an issue. Malbon, *Company*, 52, notes that she is an outsider as a Gentile and as a woman.

5   The verb used here, *rising up* (*anastas*), is adopted by Mark when Jesus embarks on a significant new activity (1:35; 10:1); see Donahue & Harrington, *Mark*, 232; Byrne, *A Costly Freedom*, 125. Boring, *Mark*, 207, observes that the verb is used of Jesus' resurrection; it is a subtle reminder of the realities of the post-Easter life of the Church. Some manuscripts add "and Sidon" (as in Matthew). Harrington, *Mark*, 104, notes that the region of Tyre included upper Galilee; Nineham, *Mark*, 200, thinks it was Gentile only in a very limited sense.

6   For example in Isa 25:22 and Ezek 27:32. Boring, *Mark*, 209, notes that Tyre is presented there as the traditional enemy of the Jews, but, because it helped in the building of the temple, it was sometimes promised a part in eschatological salvation (Ezek 26–28; Joel 3:4–8; Amos 1:9–10; Zech 9:1–4.)

7   Boring, *Mark*, 209. Tyrian coinage was used in Galilee; Tyrian troops served Rome in the devastation of Galilee. "Bread" was a potent economic symbol, as well as having theological overtones. Culpepper, *Mark*, 238, calls Galilee "the breadbasket of the region". In difficult times the wealthy Tyrians could literally buy the bread off the tables of the Jews.

8   In Matthew's version (15:21–28) they are present with Jesus and have a role in the story, urging Jesus to send away the annoying woman.

9   Hooker, *Mark*, 183.

10   Usually, this is the place where he instructs his disciples, but this time he is alone.

11   McBride, *Mark*, 118, recalls that people from that area sought Jesus out in 3:8; also, Donahue & Harrington, *Mark*, 233.

12   See 1:40 (the leper); 5:22 (Jairus) and 5:33 (the woman with the flow of blood). Donahue & Harrington, *Mark*, 233 and 237, consider that the woman is a Greek lady of some social status, a landed property owner. She is herself crossing a social barrier; "she also crosses the boundary between stereotypical male dominance and female submissiveness." Boring, *Mark*, 210, considers her a member of the wealthy urban class (the Greek words used for bed and table are an indication).

13   Some manuscripts have "daughter", others "little daughter". The girl never meets Jesus face to face.

14   Harrington, *Mark*, 104, sees her clearly as a representative of the Gentile world. Donahue & Harrington, *Mark*, 236, note several clear echoes of the Elijah and Elisha cycles in 1 Kings 17:8–24; 2 Kings 4:18–37.

15   Moloney, *Mark*, 146–147, observes that the saying, probably Jesus' own words, has the ring of a traditional proverbial saying. Culpepper, *Mark*, 238–239, suggests that the aphorism may have arisen out of hostility between Jews in Galilee and the more affluent Tyrians in connection with bread supplies in times of famine; see also Boring, *Mark*, 209. On p. 213 he points out that neither Jesus nor Mark created the metaphor.

16   Wright, *Mark*, 95. Matthew, whose version does not take place in a house, makes this explicit, for Jesus says: "I was sent only to the lost sheep of the house of Israel." Isaiah included the nations in his view of salvation history: 2:2–4; 42:1; 60:1–3; 66:18–20. Paul's later practice was to preach first to the Jews and then the Gentiles (Rom 1:16; 2:9–10; Acts 3:26; 13:46; 18:6). Donahue & Harrington, *Mark*, 233, suggest an allusion to the two feeding miracles (6:30–44; 8:1–10). Malbon, *Company*, 52, observes that Jesus' statement is undermined by his earlier healing of the Gerasene demoniac.

17   Wright, *Mark*, 95, for instance.

18   Culpepper, *Mark*, 240. Boring, *Mark*, 210–211, dismisses such views.

19   Hooker, *Mark*, 182. On p. 183, she suggests that in its present context the term is a challenge to the woman to justify her request.

20   Boring, *Mark*, 214.

21   Hooker, *Mark*, 183; Moloney, *Mark*, 147; Byrne, *A Costly Freedom*, 126. Culpepper, *Mark*, 242, sees the word as possibly a confession; Boring, 214, as an acceptance of his authority; but for the reader, it is a Christian confession. Malbon, *Mark's Jesus*, 85, notes the deliberate and significant ambiguity.

22   Non-Jews allowed dogs into their homes; they were household pets rather than mongrel scavengers. Maybe in her experience the children deliberately threw them scraps; see Martin, *Mark*, 180. Boring, *Mark*, 214, notes that in a Jewish context a dog is an outsider, whereas in a Gentile context it is an insider, a member of the family.

23   Hooker, *Mark*, 183.

24   Nineham, *Mark*, 199.

25   In Matthew, Jesus' appreciation of her faith is strongly expressed: "Great is your faith." Malbon, *Company*, 53, notes that it is her action in speaking up and speaking out (her 'word'), not her faith alone or reasoning alone, that causes Jesus to change his mind and grant her request.

26   See Malbon, *Mark's Jesus*, 134.

27   Moloney, *Mark*, 145, observes that in all the New Testament stories of Jesus curing from a distance the aspect of wonder is lacking. He adds, on p. 148, that all the stories (Matt 8:5–13; Luke 7:1–10; John 4:46–54) are the result of a Gentile request. Anderson, *Mark*, 189, notes that neither the miracle nor its effect is dwelt upon, the emphasis rests on the dialogue, the relative position of Jew and Gentile in the economy of salvation; similarly, McBride, *Mark*, 119; Nineham, *Mark*, 198; Meier, *A Marginal Jew*, 659.

28   From the perspective of the evangelist, the Gentile mission was a vibrant reality, and the Church was predominantly Gentile.

29   Hooker, *Mark*, 182.

30   Isa 49:6

31   Moloney, *Mark*, 147. Boring, *Mark*, 213, writes that the metaphor was intentionally crafted by the narrator to allow the woman to adapt it for her own

(Markan) purpose. For the present the Jewish children are being fed; later the Gentiles will be included in the messianic salvation.

32   Hooker, *Mark,* 184.

33   Donahue & Harrington, *Mark,* 237.

34   Pope Francis, *Christus Vivit,* 75, writes: "As a Church, may we never fail to weep before these tragedies of our young. May we never become inured to them, for anyone incapable of tears cannot be a mother." He wants society to learn how to be a caring mother, a promise of life. He asks: "Can I weep when I see a child who is starving, on drugs or on the street, homeless, abandoned, mistreated or exploited as a slave by society?"

35   Bartholomé, *Los Niños,* 74–75.

36   Donahue & Harrington, *Mark,* 237; Moloney, *Mark,* 147.

37   See Eph 2:14

38   Harrington, *Mark,* 105.

CHAPTER FIVE

A Father and a Suffering Son

For our next episode we will stay with Mark (9:14–29). Matthew and Luke abbreviate their versions of this story considerably (Matt 17:14–21; Luke 9:37–43a). In Mark's narrative, after the cure of the daughter of the Syro-Phoenician woman, Jesus cures a man who is deaf and dumb, feeds a crowd of 4000 with bread and fish, is involved in a controversy with some Pharisees who demand a sign from him to prove his authenticity, crosses the lake again, and, on reaching Bethsaida, cures a blind man. As well as closing one block of material, this story introduces another block, which concludes with the cure of another blind man, Bartimaeus, on the outskirts of Jericho (10:46-52). The cure of the first blind man is closely linked with the incident which follows, namely, Peter's confession of Jesus at Caesarea Philippi. The cure of the Bethsaida blind man takes place in two stages: at first, the man sees partially, and after Jesus has again laid his hands upon his eyes, his sight is fully restored. Peter's confession "You are the Messiah" shows only partial understanding; it is followed by the first of three occasions when Jesus speaks about his coming passion, death and vindication. Peter cannot accept this type of messiahship and its implications for discipleship. In the rest of this section, Jesus seeks to instruct the disciples on what discipleship really means, without much success.

A week after the discussion about his identity, Jesus takes Peter, James and John with him up a mountain, and is transfigured in their presence, his clothes becoming dazzling white. On the way down the mountain after that remarkable experience, the three disciples raise the question about Elijah's expected coming and are informed that he has already come, presumably in the person of the Baptist. On reaching the rest of the group of disciples, Jesus and his three companions encounter a scene of confusion.[1] The text reads as follows:

> When they came to the disciples, they saw a great crowd around them, and some scribes arguing with them. When the whole crowd saw him, they were immediately overcome with awe, and they ran forward to greet him. He asked them, 'What are you arguing about with them?' Someone from the crowd answered him, 'Teacher, I brought you my son; he has a spirit that makes him unable to speak; and whenever it seizes him, it dashes him down; and he foams and grinds his teeth and becomes rigid; and I asked your disciples to cast it out, but they could not do so.' He answered them, 'You faithless generation, how much longer must I be among you? How much longer must I put up with you? Bring him to me.' And they brought the boy to him. When the spirit saw him, immediately it threw the boy into convulsions, and he fell on the ground and rolled about, foaming at the mouth. Jesus asked the father, 'How long has this been happening to him?' And he said, 'From childhood. It has often cast him into the fire and into the water, to destroy him; but if you are able to do anything, have pity on us and help us.' Jesus said to him, 'If you are able! —All things can be done for the one who believes.' Immediately the father of the child cried out, 'I believe; help my unbelief!' When Jesus saw that a crowd came running together, he rebuked the unclean spirit, saying to it, 'You spirit that keep this boy from speaking and hearing, I command you, come out of him, and never enter him again!' After crying out and convulsing him terribly, it came out, and the boy was like a corpse, so that most of them said, 'He is dead.' But Jesus took him by the hand and lifted him up, and he was able to stand. When he had entered the house, his disciples asked him privately, 'Why could we not cast it out?' He said to them, 'This kind can come out only through prayer.' (9:14–29)

Jesus' disciples are in the midst of a large crowd and are discussing or even arguing with some scribes. The people have presumably been waiting for Jesus, and on catching sight of him, they excitedly rush up to greet him.[2] Jesus then asks the disciples what the argument with the scribes is all about.[3] It could well have concerned the correct procedure for exorcising demons, the authority of Jesus, or, more likely, the disciples' failure to solve the problem and remedy the situation. The question remains hanging in the air, for a man from the crowd interrupts, explaining that he has brought to Jesus his son who is possessed by a spirit of dumbness. He has come to Jesus out of a mixture of desperation and hope; clearly he has some faith in Jesus' healing power.[4] In Jesus' absence the disciples have been unable to cast the spirit out, though earlier in other cases they have succeeded in doing so (6:13). The man, addressing Jesus as "Master", gives a vivid description of the boy's plight: the spirit takes hold of him and throws him to the ground, where he foams at the mouth, grinds his teeth and goes rigid. The symptoms indicate a form of epilepsy, typically interpreted in terms of demon possession.[5] Jesus is wearied and exasperated by the lack of faith which surrounds him, especially that of his disciples,[6] but commands that the boy be brought to him. As this happens, the spirit throws the boy into convulsions. Jesus asks the boy's father how long this has been taking place and is informed that the boy has been afflicted in this way since childhood; the spirit has attempted to destroy the boy by throwing him into fire and water. The situation is manifestly serious; it must have caused deep anguish and suffering to the parents, along with the fear of losing him permanently.

The man then pleads: "But if you are able to do anything, have compassion on us and help us." In the Gospels there are many requests for mercy, but this is the only occasion when the technical term for compassion (*splanchnizesthai*) occurs as part of a request. The man appeals to the compassion of Jesus for both the boy and himself, and doubtless for family and friends too. In reply Jesus repeats the conditional ("if"), highlighting the lack of faith evident in its use, a hesitancy possibly caused by the failure of Jesus' disciples to provide help. Jesus states clearly that everything can be done (by God) for the one who trustingly believes.[7] In the first place this refers to Jesus, who trusts in God; "his immediacy with God is the source of his miraculous authority," God's power is available to him.[8] It then refers to the distraught father.[9] Acknowledging the inadequacy of his faith, he responds to Jesus' challenge with a further plea: "I believe; help my unbelief!" It is a heartfelt cry, echoed down the ages by many struggling with a wavering faith, "one of the most memorable and beloved statements in the New Testament."[10] He is torn between faith and unbelief.[11] This second request concerns himself alone. Jesus responds compassionately to both requests simultaneously.[12] With solemnity and his customary personal authority, he commands the evil spirit to depart from the boy definitively. There is a final convulsion which leaves the boy like a corpse. But Jesus takes him by the hand, and raises him up.[13] There are overtones of resurrection here; "the Christian language of resurrection rings out as the miracle story comes to a close."[14] This episode is a further example of God's victory in the cosmic struggle with evil, effected through the ministry of Jesus. There is no response from the father or the crowd, as is normally the case in the miracle story format. The story ends rather abruptly.

To the question posed by the disciples later in the house, Jesus makes it clear that it was their lack of prayer which rendered them unable to respond to the father's request and the boy's need. They were probably presuming in their own ability, becoming self-sufficient, and no longer depending on God. "Mark's community is being given a lesson on the primary place of prayer in the lives of those who follow Jesus and minister to others.... The source of all ministry, including that of Jesus, is an attitude of utter dependence on God."[15]

Reflections

In this episode we meet a frustrated Jesus. He is uncomfortable with excited crowds, disappointed with the performance of his disciples and ill at ease with the father's lack of faith. On the other hand, he is clearly moved by the man's description of the dreadful plight of his son, which he takes time to listen to. The man hit the right note in appealing to his compassion. Jesus challenges the man's hesitant faith, pushing him to go further in his trust in God's mercy and power. In response to the man's passionate prayer for deeper faith, he casts the devil from his son. This is what his mission is about. As in other stories, he then takes the boy's hand and lifts him up. The gesture and the wording are deliberately symbolic of risen life too.

The father in the story is a touching figure. One senses the depth of his anguish, his concern for the welfare of his son, the pain of his own suffering over the years. There is desperation in his appeal. His hesitancy is perhaps understandable, given the milling crowds and the ineffectiveness of the disciples' intervention. But he rises to Jesus' challenge with that beautiful plea: "help my unbelief."

We can readily identify with this father, as with Jairus earlier in the narrative. All of us have people about whom we are deeply concerned, possibly young people. We doubtless bring them to Jesus in prayer, entrusting them to his compassion. It is important that we seek to involve him in these situations. He may not bring healing in quite the way we would wish, but he will help them and us to cope better. And we make our own the father's prayer: "help my unbelief." I think that we are constantly in that situation of believing and not believing at the same time or believing and yet not fully understanding. We grapple with our doubts and questions and faltering faith. The major challenge which faces readers of the story of Jesus is highlighted in the question which he puts to Martha in John's Gospel when he goes to Bethany to raise her brother to life: "Do you believe?"[16]

Like Jesus, we are doubtless moved by the description of the boy's suffering, an affliction which he has been experiencing for years, a violent form of epilepsy with appalling effects. We wonder what must have gone through his mind as Jesus takes his hand and helps him to his feet, healed, liberated, given the opportunity of a new and normal life—and all this as a free gift. In this encounter, Jesus has transformed his life, and also the life of his family.

It must have been very difficult for the father in the story to cope with the way his son behaved when attacks took place. There are young people nowadays with severe behavioural problems of different kinds. These can be quite scary, distressing and very challenging for parents and teachers. It is often difficult to know how to deal adequately with these youngsters, and how to bring peace and wholeness. The father in the story obviously stood by his son, offered him patient support, accepted the ostracism involved, did not lose hope. We all probably know parents who show remarkable acceptance, patience and loving care for their child who may have disabilities, physical or emotional. A parent is always a parent, whatever the condition of their child, and whatever happens in their life. It is so important that we support and help them.

There are also many young people in our country and beyond who are unwell in other ways, confused, caught up perhaps in drugs, suffering from anxiety and depression, trapped in hopeless family situations, struggling with life in so many ways, without purpose and direction. They need help if they are to find healing, freedom and fuller life.[17] The story we are considering raises several issues for us to face. How sensitive are we to recognise these situations? Do we experience anything like the father's concern for his son's well-being, or Jesus' compassion for the youth in dire need? Do we summon up our energy and skills, and offer our time to respond in an effective way, making real, meaningful contact with the sufferer? Do we share with Jesus' disciples the experience of failure to ease the situation? Is this because we are not "with" Jesus, we are going it alone, trusting in our own efforts and abilities? Is it because we fail to turn to God in prayer? In this episode, Jesus makes it clear that as disciples of his, involved in ministry of any kind, we need to be people of prayer. As he says clearly in John's Gospel (15:5), "Without me you can do nothing", our efforts will not bear fruit. In order to be people of prayer, we need to be people of faith. The two go together. And we can take the young people to Jesus in prayer, seeking his compassionate help on their behalf.

Endnotes

1   Culpepper, *Mark*, 301, notes the parallel with the exorcism of the Gadarene demoniac. This demon, however, is silent. There are also parallels with the raising of Jairus' daughter. Moloney, *Mark*, 182–183, believes that elements directed at the disciples have been inserted into the traditional story of a cure, resulting in a "mixed form" of healing and teaching/instruction. This may explain the odd features. Boring, *Mark*, 276, observes that the focus is not on the exorcism but on discipleship, faith and prayer. Byrne, *A Costly Freedom*, 149, suggests that the rambling, complex nature of the story may be an indication that Mark is

relying on more than one tradition. Donahue & Harrington, *Mark*, 280, emphasise that the story is an exorcism, not a healing; however, the story is a combination of the literary forms of a healing, an exorcism and a pronouncement; also Meier, *A Marginal Jew*, 655. Harrington, *Mark*, 139, observes that just as the heavenly acknowledgement of Jesus in the baptism scene was followed by the wilderness temptation scene, so the acknowledgement at the transfiguration is followed by another encounter with a demon.

2 Some interpreters, including Hooker, *Mark*, 222–223, think there may have been something unusual about Jesus' post-transfiguration appearance, akin to that of Moses on descending from Sinai. Boring, *Mark*, 273, suggests that the crowd's amazement is mentioned here rather than at the end of the story because Mark wishes to focus there on a different point. Culpepper, *Mark*, 302, notes that the verb used to describe the crowd's reaction to Jesus really means "very excited".

3 In the text the identity of the "them" is unclear. I have opted for the disciples, though it could refer to the crowd. The scribes have no further role in the story.

4 Donahue & Harrington, *Mark*, 277–278. They suggest that the spirit which possesses the boy renders him incapable of speaking and is speechless itself. In earlier exorcisms the spirits speak (1:24; 5:7).

5 Bartholomé, *Los Niños*, 82, notes that to have a son possessed by an unclean spirit would entail social ostracism for the family; on p. 83, n. 99, he observes that epilepsy was often linked to the power of the moon; in fact, Matthew calls the child a "lunatic" (17:15). Luke 9:38 refers to him as an "only child".

6 Martin, *Mark*, 227; Moloney, *Mark*, 183, maintains that this refers to the disciples, who are in danger of drawing close to the "faithless generation" referred to in negative terms in 8:12, 15, 38. Despite the disciples' lack of faith, however, Jesus will not in fact abandon them. Culpepper, *Mark*, 304, considers them as representative of their generation. Donahue & Harrington, *Mark*, 278, detect a hint of Jesus' sense of his approaching death; also, Martin, *Mark*, 227. Boring, *Mark*, 273–274, notes that Jesus' response addresses the present situation as typifying the whole unbelieving generation with which the ministry deals. Similar phraseology expressing God's exasperation is found in Num 14:11; Deut 32:20. McBride, *Mark*, 146, comments that Jesus is wondering how long he must live among a people so spiritually dull and unsympathetic.

7 *Panta dynata (all things are possible)* occurs three times in Mark (9:23; 10:27; 14:36), and only once elsewhere in the New Testament. McBride, *Mark*, 146, notes that the issue is not whether Jesus is able, but whether the father can believe; Hooker, *Mark*, 224. Meier, *A Marginal Jew*, 655, comments that it is unusual for Jesus to demand faith as a condition for an exorcism.

8 Moloney, *Mark*, 184; for him Jesus is the model of belief; Hooker, *Mark*,224; Boring, *Mark* 274; David Rhoads, Joanna Dewey & Donald Michie, *Mark as* Story (Minneapolis: Fortress, 1999), 107. Voorwinde, *Jesus' Emotions*, 92, sees this interpretation as possible, but believes it makes more sense to see it as a challenge to the doubting man; likewise Byrne, *A Costly Freedom*, 148, n. 31, who maintains that the power which Jesus possesses is in virtue of his status as God's Son and Messiah, not in virtue of any faith relationship to God. Donahue & Harrington, *Mark*, 278,

suggest that Jesus is criticising both the disciples and the father. Martin, *Mark,* 228, opts for the father.

9   Moloney, *Mark,* 185, n. 58, sees the man as a contrast to the disciples, not as paralleling their limited faith; Mark exploits the gap between them; they do not turn to Jesus in their need. Malbon, *Mark's Jesus,* 86, believes that Jesus' words are for the disciples as much as the father.

10   Donahue & Harrington, *Mark,* 279. Malbon, *Mark's Jesus,* 86, sees the father's statement "as an emblem of the dynamic process of faith."

11   Voorwinde, *Jesus' Emotions,* 92. For Boring, *Mark,* 275, he both believes, and does not believe.

12   The reference to the gathering of a crowd, as if for the first time (despite 9:14), which spurs Jesus into action, is obscure. Voorwinde, *Jesus' Emotions,* 94, thinks that Jesus does not wish this difficult exorcism to become a public spectacle. Donahue & Harrington, *Mark,* 279, refer to the possibility of a riot. Moloney, *Mark,* 185, n. 60, suggests that it is best explained as a rearrangement of pre-Markan tradition. The crowd witnesses the miracle, but their wonder has already been reported in v.15.

13   Also 1:31 (Simon's mother-in-law); 5:41 (Jairus' daughter), where the same three verbs are used (grasped, raised, arose).

14   Moloney, *Mark,* 185; see Culpepper, *Mark,* 307; Martin, *Mark,* 230; Donahue & Harrington, *Mark,* 279–280. Voorwinde, *Jesus' Emotions,* 95, notes the two typical resurrection verbs (*egeirein, anistēmi*); the miracle is not only an exorcism but a direct pointer to the resurrection of Jesus. He quotes Lane in noting that it is through Jesus' death and resurrection that Satan's power can be definitively broken.

15   McBride, *Mark,* 147; Martin, *Mark,* 230-231. Moloney, *Mark,* 186, puts it: "They must learn to turn to God in faith and prayer if they are to hope to be successful *disciples of Jesus."*

16   John 11:26, 40.

17   Pope Francis, in *Christus Vivit,* 71–74, notes how in today's rapidly changing world the lives of many young people are exposed to suffering and manipulation. He specifies those living in war zones, where there is kidnapping, extortion, human trafficking, slavery, sexual exploitation, wartime rape. In other places some young people suffer persecution because of their faith. Some young people themselves commit acts of violence, are child soldiers, are involved in drug trafficking and terrorism. Others are taken in by ideologies.

Chapter Six

The Boy with Bread and Fishes

The story of Jesus multiplying loaves of bread and a few fish to feed the multitude is found in all four Gospels, a rare occurrence for Gospel narratives. In Mark and Matthew there are, in fact, two accounts of Jesus' multiplying activity, one in which the recipients number 5000, the other in which the clientele is slightly smaller, numbering 4000.[1] In general, scholars maintain that the second story is probably an alternative version or 'doublet' of the first, rather than a separate incident in the ministry of Jesus. Luke and John have just a single version. It is John's presentation which I propose to consider in this chapter.[2]

John's way of telling the story of Jesus is very different from that of the other three evangelists. He begins with a poetic piece, usually referred to as the Prologue, in which he speaks about the Word, who was with God before time began, was involved in the world's creation, and became flesh, a human being, with the name Jesus. The story proper commences with the witness of the Baptist, which leads two of his disciples to go after Jesus and transfer their allegiance to him, quickly involving others in the venture. The evangelist structures the next section of his story between two incidents which take place in Cana: the wedding in which Jesus changes water into wine, and the cure of the official's son. Within this bracket, Jesus holds a discussion with Nicodemus, an important religious leader, and then with the woman of Samaria. In the Cana to Cana section, the evangelist is exploring the issue of faith response to Jesus. The next major block of material is structured around the Jewish liturgical feasts: Sabbath, Passover, Tabernacles and Dedication. The subsequent raising to life of Lazarus is the catalyst for the passion and death of Jesus.

The story of the multiplication of loaves and fishes occurs after the Sabbath discussions, and is a prelude to the discourse on the bread of life. It reads as follows:

> After this Jesus went to the other side of the Sea of Galilee, also called the Sea of Tiberias. A large crowd kept following him, because they saw the signs that he was doing for the sick. Jesus went up the mountain and sat down there with his disciples. Now the Passover, the festival of the Jews, was near. When he looked up and saw a large crowd coming towards him, Jesus said to Philip, 'Where are we to buy bread for these people to eat?' He said this to test him, for he himself knew what he was going to do. Philip answered him, 'Six months' wages would not buy enough bread for each of them to get a little.' One of his disciples, Andrew, Simon Peter's brother, said to him, 'There is a boy here who has five barley loaves and two fish. But what are they among so many people?' Jesus said, 'Make the people sit down.' Now there was a great deal of grass in the place; so they sat down, about five thousand in all. Then Jesus took the loaves, and when he had given thanks, he distributed them to those who were seated; so also the fish, as much as they wanted. When they were satisfied, he told his disciples, 'Gather up the fragments left over, so that nothing may be lost.' So they gathered them up, and from the fragments of the five barley loaves, left by those who had eaten, they filled twelve baskets. When the people saw the sign that he had done, they began to say, 'This is indeed the prophet who is to come into the world.' When Jesus realized that they were about to come and take him by force to make him king, he withdrew again to the mountain by himself. (6:1–15)

The setting for the story is Galilee. It is now close to the time of the great pilgrim feast of Passover.[3] Two original feasts, the Passover, which entailed the sacrifice of a lamb amongst a pastoral people, and Unleavened Bread, a barley harvest festival amongst sedentary farmers, had been amalgamated and historicised to remember the Exodus event. Families celebrated a festal meal with a lamb, unleavened bread and herbs. Key elements from the dramatic journey through the wilderness were recalled: the crossing of the sea of reeds, the manna and quails, the thirst and supply of water, the Sinai covenant and gift of the Law, the birth of the nation of Israel as God's chosen people. Obviously, a key figure in all this was the person of Moses.[4] It is this reference to Passover which provides the background and theological key for the whole episode.[5]

Jesus takes a brief boat journey across the lake. John is alone amongst the evangelists in calling this stretch of water the Sea of Tiberias.[6] Jesus is "followed" by a crowd, enthusiastic because of the impressive signs he has wrought in curing people who were sick. Such enthusiasm, the reader knows, can prove suspect and problematic. Jesus climbs the hillside and sits with his disciples.[7]

The tradition behind John's version of the story has been coloured, I believe, by two factors: an episode in the book of Kings, and the celebration of the Eucharist as experienced in the Johannine community.[8] The former reads as follows:

> A man came from Baal-shalishah, bringing food from the first fruits to the man of God: twenty loaves of barley and fresh ears of grain in his sack. Elisha said, 'Give it to the people and let them eat.' But his servant said, 'How can I set this before a hundred people?' So he repeated, 'Give it to the people and let them eat, for thus says the Lord, "They shall eat and have some left."' He set it before them, they ate, and had some left, according to the word of the Lord. (2 Kings 4:42–44).

Imagine coming from Baal-shalishah, a name to die for, so much more exciting and inspirational than my hometown of Wigan! There are several obvious points of contact between the two narratives.[9] There are two available items of food, (loaves and grain, bread and fish). The prophet gives a command, his servant hesitates, the prophet insists. The same occurs with Jesus and the two disciples, as he poses the question, and they struggle to face the reality of the situation in which they are involved, focusing on practicalities.[10] There are the leftovers, and the explicit reference to barley loaves (only John has barley loaves[11]). But most fascinating is the fact that in John it is a boy who provides the loaves and fishes, not the disciples. The term which John uses to describe him, the diminutive term *paidarion*, is often applied to a young slave, male or female, but it is the word used to designate the servant of Elisha in the story mentioned above (also in 2 Kings 4:12, 14, 25; 5:20). It appeals to me as a Salesian of Don Bosco that it is a young person who plays such a key role in the story. He offers what he has, and although it is not much, Jesus uses it to feed the multitude. They have as much as they want. There is a great deal left over, which Jesus tells his disciples to gather up.

In the Johannine text it is Jesus, not the disciples, who takes the initiative in responding to the crowd, concerned that they should be fed. He raises the issue with Philip, who considers the provision of food expensive and realistically impossible; Andrew's sceptical reference to the meagre supplies of the boy shows that he, too, has not understood. "The food of Jesus belongs to another level of reality."[12] Jesus makes the people recline on the springtime grass, a clear indication that they will be fed, and perhaps an echo of Psalm 23 and the shepherd theme. The central action is described simply.[13] Jesus, as the host, takes the loaves, gives thanks to God, and distributes the bread. John uses the verb *eucharistein*. There is no reference to his breaking the bread. He then does the same with the fish. It is Jesus alone who, as host, distributes food for everyone without any assistance from the disciples.[14] He is the unique provider. The guests have as much as they want; they are well and truly satisfied, for there are twelve baskets of fragments left over.[15] Jesus then instructs his disciples to gather up the leftovers so that nothing will be lost, using a verb which is found in Exodus for the daily gathering of the manna.[16] There is no mention of the fish here; the focus is on the bread. The scraps are much more plentiful than the original outlay.

The crowd react to the feeding enthusiastically, voicing an assessment that Jesus is the prophet who is to come into the world, a further hint of the Moses tradition.[17] With a further interesting mixture of understanding and misunderstanding, the people interpret the feeding as a kingly act, and so they attempt by force to proclaim Jesus as their messianic king. Jesus is uncomfortable with this inadequate, misguided and dangerous perception, and beats a hasty retreat, escaping to the hills.

The original incident behind John's narrative may have been intended by Jesus as a symbolic gesture, a sign that the messianic era was dawning, the dreams and hopes of centuries were being fulfilled, the joy and plenty expected to characterise God's saving intervention had arrived. The banquet imagery and the idea of messianic abundance are features of the earlier Cana story also, when Jesus provides 120 gallons of wine for the wedding party.[18] Those hearing or reading the story later would inevitably connect it with their own community celebration of the Eucharist, through which the risen Jesus draws them, draws us too, further into the new era which he has introduced.

The following day the people meet up with Jesus and there is some dialogue about bread, which leads into a discourse of Jesus. The people recall the Exodus stories of Moses providing food for them whilst they were in the wilderness, bread from heaven. Jesus claims that he himself is the Bread from heaven, a source of nourishment which satisfies our human hunger in an entirely new way, far beyond what Moses could offer in the manna of the desert experience. In the earlier part of the discourse, bread refers to the revelation which Jesus brings. For, in Jewish circles the image of manna was often used to denote instruction, divine word, or wisdom. The rabbis interpreted it as the Law, a source of revelation and life. The Old Testament often presents divine word or wisdom under the symbol of bread. The highpoint of this revelation takes place in the self-giving of Jesus when the "hour" has come, and the Son of Man is "lifted up" on Calvary's hill, and as the Good Shepherd, gives his life for the sheep.

As the discourse proceeds, Jesus introduces a new element, as he proclaims: "The bread that I shall give for the life of the world is my flesh." And he continues by telling his audience that if they eat his flesh and drink his blood, they shall have eternal life, they shall live in him and he in them, and shall be raised on the last day. The language is unmistakably eucharistic: bread, bread which is flesh, blood, the invitation to eat and also to drink, giving, for the world. When the Christian community celebrates the Eucharist, the "hour" of Jesus is made present again. Some scholars suggest that instead of including the words over the bread and the cup during the supper, this evangelist filled the gap with the washing of the disciples' feet by Jesus. That gesture, like the Synoptic breaking of the bread, points to his self-giving in death. But Jesus also makes it a model for the way in which we, his disciples, relate to and treat one another. John, therefore, is indicating that liturgical celebration cannot be divorced from daily living. We are challenged to make real in our daily lives the self-giving, love and service of Jesus. We are called and sent to live Eucharist, to be Eucharist.

Reflections

Alongside the profound meaning of this story and the subsequent discourse, there is, I believe, a further message which must not be overlooked: the role of the young boy. He could have been present amongst the crowd with family and friends, but he is carrying with him his own food supplies, suggesting a level of independence. This he generously donates to Jesus, with that kind of generosity which young people are often capable of showing. We are not told of the interaction between him and Jesus as he hands his food over, nor of his reaction when he sees Jesus feed thousands with his meagre supplies. Like the Samaritan woman with her water, he responds to Jesus' need, and Jesus is happy to receive what he offers. There is a wonderful openness and humility about Jesus, a willingness to depend on others.

And in this there is a lesson for us all. Young people can be generous, thoughtful, outgoing and kind; they willingly respond to situations of need. At times they show amazing creativity in fundraising ventures, and in other ways of volunteering. They can suggest new ideas, new possibilities, new ways of viewing and doing things, and provide a welcome injection of enthusiasm and energy. They have much to offer the older generation. They can also do things which adults cannot do. It was always Don Bosco's style to harness this potential for good, involving them in service and mission. For us adults, it is important, first, to believe in their capacity for generosity, and, secondly, to welcome their offers and create opportunities, and then to encourage, challenge and support them in their response, helping them to grow. The ability to forget self and reach out to others in service and care is a fundamental aspect of being a follower of Jesus.

I recently read a story in which a young girl is dying of an illness from which her older brother, now eight years of age, has previously been cured. The doctor tells him that only if he donates his blood for a transfusion can his sister be saved. At this suggestion, the boy becomes afraid. After a brief pause, however, he agrees. An hour after the transfusion has taken place, the boy fearfully asks the doctor when he is going to die. The doctor then realises that when the boy agreed to give his blood, he thought it meant that he would give his life for his sister. Yet, he had said "yes".[19]

The generosity of the young can be a reminder for us that, as followers of Jesus, we, too, are called to be generous people. Later in his narrative, the evangelist John recounts the incident at the home of Lazarus and his sisters. During a celebratory meal, Mary anoints the feet of Jesus with some very expensive and fragrant perfume, as an expression of her love and care. In Mark's version of this episode, the unnamed woman who anoints Jesus breaks open her alabaster jar, emptying it completely (14:3–9). Shortly before this, a widow has placed a couple of small copper coins, almost worthless, into the treasury containers at the Temple. This Jesus notices, and points it out to his disciples: "Out of her poverty, she has put in everything that she had, all she had to live on" (12:41–44). The stories take place in what we now call Holy Week, and they set the scene for Jesus' generosity in giving everything to and for us on Calvary. Today we remember and are caught up in this generous self-giving whenever we celebrate Eucharist.

Endnotes

1 Mark 6:35–44; 8:1–10; Matt 14:13–21; 15:32–39; Luke 9:12–17; John 6:1–15

2 Meier, *A Marginal Jew*, 2:950–956, compares the versions of Mark and John, concluding that John's version is a tradition similar to but not literarily dependent on the version of the story preserved in Mark 6 and 8. See Raymond E. Brown, *The Gospel according to John*, 2 vols. (London: Chapmans, 1972), 1:236–250; Culpepper, *Gospel and Letters*, 154. Francis J. Moloney, *The Gospel of John*. Sacra Pagina 4. (Collegeville, MN: Glazier, 1998), 197, notes that a unique Johannine point of view has been insinuated into the telling of the traditional story. C. Kingsley Barrett, *The*

Gospel according to John, 2nd ed. (London: SPCK, 1978), 226, on the other hand, believes that John knew the two versions in Mark; Andrew T. Lincoln, *The Gospel according to Saint John* (Grand Rapids, MI: Baker Academic, 2005), 216, holds that John has reworked Mark 6.

3   Chapters 5–10 of the Fourth Gospel explore the relationship between the old Jewish feasts and the new age introduced by Jesus; Jesus brings the Jewish Passover to fulfilment, and gives it new meaning, here especially the bread/manna aspect, and later in the Gospel, the lamb.

4   See G.A. Yee, *Jewish Feasts and the Gospel of John* (Collegeville, MN: Liturgical Press, 1989), 60–65; Moloney, *John,* 194.

5   Charles H. Dodd, *The Interpretation of the Fourth Gospel* (Cambridge: CUP, 1968), 300, sees the Passover reference as a hint of the eucharistic significance that the narrative will reveal; Barrett, *John,* 228.

6   Also 21:1. Biblical writers tend to call any body of water (other than rivers) a "sea". Herod completed the building of the lakeside town in the twenties CE and dedicated it to the emperor; the use of the name also for the lake probably occurred later in the century after the time of Jesus; see Brown, *John,* 1:232; Barrett, *John,* 227.

7   Francis J. Moloney, *Living Voice of the Gospel* (Dublin: Veritas, 2006), 279, sees this as a hint that Jesus is adopting a position parallel to Moses who received the Law on a mountain. See Brown, *John,* 1:232; Lincoln, *John,* 211; Giorgio Zevini, *Vangelo secondo Giovanni,* 2 vols. (Rome: Città Nuova, 1998), 1:222.

8   See Meier, *A Marginal Jew,* 2:958–967.

9   Meier, *A Marginal Jew,* 2:960–961; Brown, *John,* 1:246; Barrett, *John,* 229.

10   The response of Philip recalls Num 11:13.

11   Culpepper, *Gospel and Letters,* 156, observes that barley ripened earlier than wheat, and since it was cheaper, it was used for bread by the poor; Brown, *John,* 1:233, also notes that three loaves were looked on as a meal for one person. Lincoln, *John,* 212, acknowledges the verbal links with the Elisha story, commenting that the amount used by Jesus is smaller and the number of participants greater.

12   Barnabas Lindars, *The Gospel of John* (London: Oliphants, 1972), 241.

13   Brendan Byrne, *Life Abounding* (Strathfield NSW: St Pauls Publications, 2014), 112, detects echoes of the Synoptic accounts of the institution of the Eucharist. Lincoln, *John,* 212, comments that the language recalls that used in the early Church's eucharistic practice; Brown, *John,* 1:247: "the wording of the multiplication accounts was coloured by the eucharistic liturgies familiar in the various communities"; Lindars, *John,* 242.

14   Moloney, *John,* 198, comments that the distribution of the loaves recalls the formal setting of the eucharistic celebration. Barrett, *John,* 230, notes that the words and actions of Jesus recall the Last Supper.

15   Byrne, *Life Abounding,* 112, sees the reference to twelve baskets as the first indication in this Gospel of a select group of twelve making up the inner core of Jesus' disciples; this is rendered explicit at the end of the chapter; see Lincoln, *John,* 213.

16   Exod 16:8–21. The manna was not to be stored; what remained, decayed. The verb is also used in the early Church for the gathering of the community, and the gathering up of the eucharistic fragments. Some scholars see the influence of the community's celebration of the Eucharist on the wording of the narrative: Passover and Eucharistic blend. See Brown, *John,* 1:247; Moloney, *John,* 198; Meier, *A Marginal Jew,* 2:963; Lindars, *John,* 243. Brown, *John,* 1:248, concludes: "the eucharistic coloring of the Johannine account of the multiplication seems beyond doubt."

17   Deut 18:15–18: Yahweh's promise to raise up a prophet like Moses.

18   Another background strand is the dreaming of the prophets as they looked forward to a new age of God's saving closeness, and often used the image of a banquet at which the Messiah would preside. The time of God's decisive intervention would be characterised by plentiful supplies of food and wine; see Isa 25:6; 55:1f; 65:13f; Joel 3:18; Amos 9:13. These texts can be applied also to the wedding in Cana (John 2:1–11).

19   Bruno Ferrero, *La Cena in Paradiso* (Turin: Elledici, 2016), 33.

CHAPTER SEVEN

The Markan Children

In the Synoptic tradition there are two episodes in which Jesus is directly involved with young children; both encounters also become the occasion of important pieces of teaching about discipleship. Following the Markan version, the first meeting takes place in the narrative soon after Jesus has cast out the evil spirit from the boy at the request of his distraught father, the incident which we considered in the last chapter. Jesus has again spoken about his coming passion, but the disciples have once more failed to understand, and are said to have been afraid to pursue the issue further.[1] Jesus and the disciples have subsequently made their way back to Capernaum.

The First Encounter

The story continues:

> Then they came to Capernaum; and when he was in the house he asked them, 'What were you arguing about on the way?' But they were silent, for on the way they had argued with one another about who was the greatest. He sat down, called the twelve, and said to them, 'Whoever wants to be first must be last of all and servant of all.' Then he took a little child and put it among them; and taking it in his arms, he said to them, 'Whoever welcomes one such child in my name welcomes me, and whoever welcomes me welcomes not me but the one who sent me.' (9:33-37)

The very human issue of status, rank, control, prestige and honour, relevant in that culture and society, and, it would seem, in their own group, is troubling the disciples.[2] Jesus has noticed that something was in the air as they walked along.[3] Now that they are back in the house in Capernaum, presumably that of Peter, his question about the topic of their arguing on the road makes them uncomfortable and embarrassed. Jesus responds to their ensuing heavy but eloquent silence with a very clear statement, subverting their perspectives, and highlighting the inappropriate nature of their discussion after he had again spoken about his passion. The one aiming to be first must be last, and must see himself as servant of all, with no exceptions. That really does give them something to ponder![4]

Jesus' words are reinforced by a symbolic gesture, as, sitting down as a teacher, he takes a child in his arms with warmth and kindness, showing genuine affection, respect and care. In that culture, a child was lacking in status and legal rights, was a non-person, totally dependent on others. Kindness to a child did not bring any social or material benefit. Usually rabbis did not associate with children.[5] Neither a servant nor a child has claims to power or status. For Jesus, however, insignificant people, weak members of the community, folk who are easily overlooked by those seeking power and status, people considered 'nobodies', the "last of all", have great importance.[6] His way, which must become the disciples' way, is to accept, welcome and serve those who are weak, vulnerable and in need. The verb "receive" or "welcome" is clearly crucial here. In fact, the children actually represent him, he says, they mediate his presence.[7] "It is the Risen Christ who is met in the child."[8] This reflects a very different mindset from that exhibited by the disciples, a mindset which they will continue to struggle to accept.

The Second Encounter

The second Markan episode occurs a little later in his narrative. Jesus has rebuked his disciple John for attempting to stop an exorcist who was not a formal member of the group, for "Whoever is not against us is for us." He has then spoken strongly about anyone putting a stumbling block before any of the "little ones" who believe in him. After this, Jesus moves from there to a place beyond the Jordan and teaches the people who crowded round him, "as was his custom". Some Pharisees then arrive on the scene, seeking to test him with a question about divorce. Back in the house, Jesus gives a further explanation on the topic to his disconcerted disciples. At this point:[9]

> People were bringing little children to him in order that he might touch them; and the disciples spoke sternly to them. But when Jesus saw this, he

was indignant and said to them, 'Let the little children come to me; do not stop them; for it is to such as these that the kingdom of God belongs. Truly I tell you, whoever does not receive the kingdom of God as a little child will never enter it.' And he took them up in his arms, laid his hands on them, and blessed them. (10:13–16)[10]

This is the first time that Mark mentions that "people", presumably parents or relatives, were bringing young children to Jesus.[11] The purpose of this was that he might touch them. Touch has been an aspect of Jesus' earlier healing ministry. Here it is probably linked with the idea of a blessing (Gen 48:14–16).[12] I suspect that this kind of occasion must have occurred repeatedly in Jesus' ministry, when once his reputation grew as a prophet and wonderworker. Over recent decades we have seen many photos of Pope St John Paul II and Pope Francis blessing children at their parents' behest. It is still a natural request to make of someone considered a 'man of God'. Clearly it means a lot to them.

On this occasion the disciples seek to prevent them, "speaking sternly to them."[13] Maybe they think Jesus is too weary, too busy or too important to bother with insignificant children. But Jesus has a decidedly alternative view. He is annoyed with his disciples,[14] whose attitude shows that they are not on the same wavelength as he, confirming the lack of understanding shown in previous incidents. Jesus takes a very different stance, forbidding them from such preventive action, and urging them to allow the children near.[15] Again, Jesus is operating counterculturally. His attitude is also affirming for their mothers or wider family who brought them. He takes the children in his arms affectionately, lays his hand on them and gives them a blessing.[16]

He uses the opportunity for teaching, too, affirming solemnly ("Amen") that the Kingdom belongs to such as these, people with little or no status, people on the margins, the poor, the vulnerable.[17] The aspect of childhood highlighted here is receptivity; children receive everything as a gift, usually smiling with delight; they are totally dependent on others for life's necessities (like food and clothing), for attention, affirmation and for survival. Here they serve as role models for adults and for genuine disciples. For, entry into the Kingdom of God is not a right or an achievement; it has nothing to do with status, pretensions, rank, or entitlement. It is not earned or merited, but is a free gift, the expression of God's boundless goodness, and must be received and accepted with thanks as a gift.

That the disciples continue to struggle with these revolutionary ideas of Jesus becomes even more evident later, when the two sons of Zebedee approach Jesus on the quiet, seeking the top jobs in the Kingdom. Naturally, the other disciples are put out by this one-upmanship, and make their anger evident. "So Jesus called them and said to them, 'You know that among the Gentiles those whom they recognise as their rulers lord it over them, and their great ones are tyrants over them. But it is not so among you; but whoever wishes to become great among you must be your servant, and whoever wishes to be first among you must be slave of all. For the Son of Man came not to be served but to serve, and to give his life a ransom for many'" (10:42–45). The stories of the children, then, offer a powerful and challenging illustration of the meaning of discipleship.

Reflections

Taken together, the two stories reveal Jesus as a warm, affectionate and genuinely human person. He is very much at home with children. He clearly values them and holds them in respect and esteem. He is comfortable in their company, and they in his. His hugs and blessings are natural and sincere. In this he breaks away from the cultural norm. He also reveals the mind and heart of God, his Father. At the same time, these encounters in which children are at the centre serve as catalysts, enabling Jesus to highlight two central aspects of his message and way of discipleship. They become symbols or models of the new world which he is introducing, the Kingdom of God.

The first key message, responding to the discussion of the disciples on the road, is the need to replace attitudes and styles of power, prestige and ambition by humility and generous service. Greatness takes on a completely different connotation. The verb translated as "receive" or "welcome" (*dechomai*) is mentioned in the text several times. All disciples of Jesus, not least those in any form of leadership, must see themselves as servants, and go out of their way to welcome and serve especially the young and the vulnerable.[18] Such a mindset, such a way of being and of relating are so countercultural, so foreign to the normal way we humans think and organise ourselves at all levels. Modern disciples struggle in this area of life no less than the original twelve. A radical and ongoing conversion is required. What is more, according to Jesus, receiving or welcoming a child means receiving him personally. For they represent him and mediate his presence, and they point to the Father, the One who sent him. This can stimulate our motivation and generosity.

In the second story receptivity takes on a different significance. The emphasis now is on the child's receptivity and dependence, the child's need for others. It is true that infants and children can be self-centred and difficult at times, and Jesus would know this from his village experience, but his point is that they cannot earn what they need; they are passive and powerless; they receive everything as gift, and usually delight in it; they can only give trust and affection in response. For us, this means realising, first, that we do not win our salvation by our own efforts, skills, status, position in society or church. God's acceptance, love, forgiveness, life (the Kingdom in the Synoptics, 'eternal life' in John) come to us as a free and gracious gift, unbelievably abundant. Like a child, with simplicity, wonder and joy, we can only be open to receive. Understanding this, living in this way, can be quite a challenge for us in today's world. Jesus is again turning the world upside down! God's ways are clearly not our ways. It encourages us to place our trust in God, to acknowledge our dependence on God, to place our lives with confidence into God's gracious hands.

Further, openness can be an impetus to maintain and develop a contemplative dimension in our lives. Even as adults, we can experience the wonder, curiosity, excitement of children in noticing, discovering and exploring our world. It is natural to experience delight, wonder, awe and joy in connection with the natural world, human beings, inventions, music… . Sometimes we miss these 'wow' moments because we are too busy, depressed and worried, stuck in routines. And yet, awareness and sensitivity to the multitudinous facets of our experience can lead to contemplation, to the glimpsing of a deeper dimension of it all, the presence of God. There is an intimate connection between God and what is ordinary.[19]

The role of the disciples in the second story reminds us of the danger of putting obstacles in the way of the growth and development of young people, and other vulnerable people too. Elsewhere, Jesus speaks strongly about being stumbling blocks for others (Matt 18:6–9). The child abuse scandal in the Church has painfully highlighted this danger and problem. Our role is to enable them to encounter Jesus, not prevent them from doing so. We might also examine whether we tend to close our eyes to those whom our society ignores or exploits. There are so many children who are undernourished physically and/or emotionally, and who receive little love. In the immediate context of our lives, our locality, there are the sick and infirm, the elderly, refugees, those out of work or on the streets, those struggling financially, the bereaved and lonely. As followers of Jesus we are called to reach out to these, whom Jesus calls the "little ones", with care and compassion, for they are very dear to our God, the apple of God's eye. We need to make sure that we don't take advantage of people who are in any way weaker than ourselves.

Jesus also exhorts us to seek out those in our community who may have strayed. People drift away from the church for all kinds of reasons. Sometimes "stumbling blocks" have been placed in their way by fellow Christians, by people with pastoral or educational responsibility, by harshness and lack of flexibility and understanding by clergy. Sometimes, rules and laws can control access to Jesus, and exclude rather than embrace and draw in.[20] Many have been deeply hurt. They need to find the compassionate face of God in us. Pope Francis has frequently urged us to reach out to them like the shepherd in the parable.

Endnotes

1   There are three passion predictions; each time the disciples show that they fail to understand and accept what Jesus says; each is then followed by some teaching about discipleship.

2   Boring, *Mark,* 280, states: "The discussion of relative rank within the group of disciples is not merely a matter of their personal egos, but reflects the conventions of Hellenistic society in which status and honour were very important." He also suggests that arguments about leadership were rife in the churches for which Mark writes, an issue raised also by Hooker, *Mark,* 227. Culpepper, *Mark,* 311, writes: "Rank and status were important in antiquity, and social order depended on establishing one's position and that of others". Donahue & Harrington, *Mark,* 284, suggest that the topic would have been both natural and worth discussing. Martin, *Mark,* 235, notes that to be "first" was to be top man, the head of the pecking order. The saying about first and last is found in different contexts in the Gospels; Mark has chosen to locate it here. Matthew omits the argument about greatness prior to this episode.

3   "On the way" is a reminder of the journey context, Jesus' road to Jerusalem, to suffering and death; in such a context the difference between Jesus' mindset and that of the disciples is highlighted. Mark often uses the "house" as the place where Jesus instructs the disciples.

4   McBride, *Mark,* 149, states that "ambition is redefined as a reversal of conventional wisdom." Several commentators, including Culpepper, *Mark,* 310, note that the Aramaic word *talya* can refer to both servant and child, so Jesus' action serves as an acted out parable in support of his call to the disciples to be servants; he speaks of a servant whilst holding the child. In Luke (9:46–48), Jesus is aware of the nature of the argument on the journey, and so does not ask the disciples. Jesus speaks the logion about welcome, adding "for the least among all of you is the greatest." In Matthew (18:1-5) there is no discussion on the road; instead the disciples openly ask who is the greatest in the kingdom of heaven. In reply Jesus places a child in their midst and states: "Truly I tell you, unless you change and become like children, you will never enter the kingdom of heaven. Whoever becomes humble like this child is the greatest in the kingdom of heaven. Whoever welcomes one such child in my name welcomes me." Matthew then includes words of Jesus about being a stumbling block for little ones, which leads into the parable of the lost sheep (18:10–14).

5   Donahue & Harrington, *Mark,* 285; Culpepper, *Mark,* 312. Boring, *Mark,* 281, also notes that a characteristic of a child was not innocence. Culpepper, *Mark,* 312, calls Jesus' action revolutionary in first-century Galilee; rabbis did not associate with children. In Ancient Judaism children were thought to be self-willed, lacking in understanding, and in need of stern discipline (Isa 3:4; Eccl 10:16; Wis 12:24; 15:14). See Moloney, *Mark,* 188, n. 76. The Greek term used here and in Matthew and Luke is *paidion.*

6   McBride, *Mark,* 149, comments that the scene dramatises the inclusiveness of the new community that welcomes the insignificant into its centre. Moloney, *Mark,* 188, notes that the verb "receive" is used four times in 9:37; see Hooker, *Mark,* 228, also.

7   Donahue & Harrington, *Mark,* 285, comment that in that culture the expectation was that emissaries would be treated with the respect and dignity appropriate to the one doing the sending.

8   Boring, *Mark,* 281.

9   Culpepper, *Mark,* 332, notes that Mark's sequence is not random; there is a natural connection from speaking about marriage to speaking about children. Later the issue of wealth is raised (see the following chapter); in these three episodes Jesus severely challenges the disciples' ideas on key topics.

10   Matt 19:13–15; Luke 18:15–17. In Matthew the purpose of those bringing the children is that "he might lay his hands on them and pray." He omits Jesus' saying about receiving the Kingdom as a child.

11   The Greek word used here is *paidia,* which can refer to children of any age from infancy to twelve years old (Donahue & Harrington, *Mark,* 299); also Culpepper, *Mark,* 332; Martin, *Mark,* 253; Anderson, *Mark,* 245. Moloney, *Mark,* 196, notes that the children are past infancy but not yet assuming adult responsibility, and are therefore still dependent. Luke here uses *brephē,* which means infants.

12   The custom of blessing children is referred to in the Old Testament (Gen 9:26–27; 27:28–29; 48:14–16) and the literature of the Second Temple period (Sir 3:9), and is common in Jewish families today: see Young, *Jesus, the Jewish Theologian,* 27. Martin, *Mark,* 253, reminds us that the ancient practice was to lay hands on someone's head whilst blessing them.

13   The Greek verb (*kōlyein*) can mean verbal or physical prevention. "Do not prevent" (*mē kōluete*) is also used concerning the unauthorised exorcist in 9:39. Moloney, *Mark,* 197, n. 130, quotes Grundmann (*Markus,* 206), that the disciples' response was accepted practice, both culturally and religiously. The verb is strong (*epitimaō*), indicating a strong emotional reaction on the part of the disciples: anger, indignation. It is used of Peter in his attempt to deter Jesus from his messianic path of suffering in 8:32, and of Jesus in responding to Peter in the following verse.

14   The verb used of Jesus (*aganakteō*), indicating irritation, indignation, is used of Jesus only here in the Gospels. Mark portrays Jesus' emotions, whereas Matthew and Luke tend to suppress such references, as here with regard to his indignation.

15   Later in the story, people (probably including the disciples) seek to deter blind Bartimaeus from seeking Jesus' help, and Jesus insists the he should be allowed to come to him, and gives him back his sight (10:46–52).

16   Donahue & Harrington, *Mark*, 300, say: "The embrace or 'hug' indicates Jesus' loving acceptance of the child as a model of receptiveness vis-à-vis the kingdom of God." On p. 301, "He takes children seriously as human persons, calls attention to the wisdom they display in regarding everything as a gift, and seals his genuine affection for them with an embrace and a blessing." In the Greco-Roman world there was no interest in the romantic notion of children as innocent or unspoilt creatures. See Harrington, *Mark*, 156–157; Martin, *Mark*, 255. Meier, *Matthew*, 201, describes children as "pieces of property without any rights; powerless to defend themselves, they had to rely totally on others." Boring, *Mark*, 289, says that in the Hellenistic world religiously they were non-entities.

17   Several commentators are of the opinion that v.15, regarding the kingdom, was originally a separate saying (omitted in Matthew's parallel passage but included in Matt 18:3).

18   Pope Francis, *Christus Vivit,* 14, writes: "let us also keep in mind that Jesus had no use for adults who looked down on the young or lorded it over them... . For him age did not establish privileges, and being young did not imply lesser worth or dignity."

19   See Brian Grogan, *Finding God in a Leaf: The Mysticism of Laudato Si'* (Dublin: Messenger Publications, 2018).

20   Pope Francis, in *Christus Vivit,* 40–42, with great honesty and openness discusses these issues. He takes up this topic again in the section from 95–102, entitled 'Ending Every Form of Abuse', highlighting the abuse of power, the abuse of conscience, sexual and financial abuse. He also mentions the plague of clericalism.

Chapter Eight

The Wealthy Young Man

The next episode which I propose to consider occurs in Mark's Gospel immediately after Jesus has blessed the children, the story which we have just reflected on. The person approaching Jesus in Mark's version is referred to simply as a male (*heis, someone*). Matthew follows him in this, but later in his recounting of the incident he calls him a *neaniskos,* a young man. Luke describes him as a "ruler".[1] In common parlance and understanding it is a combination of the nouns used in Matthew and Luke which prevails when considering this story: "The Rich Young Man" or "The Rich Young Ruler". I prefer Mark's version of the episode, and will focus on that, but will accept Matthew's insight about his youth, so that it clearly fits the scheme of this book.

> As he was setting out on a journey, a man ran up and knelt before him, and asked him, 'Good Teacher, what must I do to inherit eternal life?' Jesus said to him, 'Why do you call me good? No one is good but God alone. You know the commandments: "You shall not murder; You shall not commit adultery; You shall not steal; You shall not bear false witness; You shall not defraud; Honour your father and mother." ' He said to him, 'Teacher, I have kept all these since my youth.' Jesus, looking at him, loved him and said, 'You lack one thing; go, sell what you own, and give the money to the poor, and you will have treasure in heaven; then come, follow me.' When he heard this, he was shocked and went away grieving, for he had many possessions.

Jesus is moving on from the scene with the children, continuing his way to Jerusalem, when a young man runs up to him and kneels before him.[2] There is an urgency and an unusual effusiveness in his approach. He addresses Jesus as

"Good teacher", a title which is rare in Jewish literature. Some commentators suggest that along with customary respect for a rabbi, there is an element of flattery here, or maybe the man is trying a little too hard. Others opine that he is sincere and has a genuine admiration for Jesus.[3] He then poses his question: "What must I do to inherit eternal life?"[4] He exhibits the mentality of achieving entry into the Kingdom of God by dint of personal effort, or earning a future reward by performing well now in the present.[5] From the previous incident, with its stress on receptivity, the reader knows that entry into the Kingdom comes as a gift, not an achievement.

Jesus is ill at ease with the young man's words, and he reacts by asking why he has addressed him in those terms, for in Jewish thinking only God is good (Rom 7:18). This response has created interpretive problems for a very long time (as far back as Matthew!).[6] The statement about God's goodness probably stems from the piety of the psalms, where one frequently finds the affirmation that God is good (Ps 53:6; 72:1; 134:3; 135:1; 117:1ff). It is a recognised truth. Jesus considers the term appropriate only for God and wishes the focus to be on God rather than on himself. Jesus is not disclaiming goodness, nor confessing sinfulness, but acknowledging his devotion to God.[7]

In moving on to answer his question, Jesus lists the commandments, aware that his interlocutor would know them well (Exod 20:1–17; Deut 5:6–21). Most Jews would be of the view that keeping these would be the route to eternal life. Jesus omits the commandments which directly refer to God, and emphasises those which deal with relationships with others, couched in negative terms, changing the order of the Decalogue, and substituting defrauding or depriving others (*apostereō*) for covetousness:[8] avoid murder, adultery, stealing, false witness and defrauding, and, positively, honour parents. The young man now addresses Jesus respectfully as "Teacher", and claims to have observed all these since his earliest days, since he became an adult.[9] This is not an arrogant boast; the young man is sincere; but perhaps it is also an indication that he believes there is something missing; he suspects that there may be more to strive for, which Jesus can indicate.

Jesus is impressed with the integrity of his life, and looks intensely at him with love, recognising the idealism, generosity and goodness in him.[10] There is indeed much more that he can do, for love of neighbour transcends the negative prescriptions of the Decalogue. With five imperatives Jesus responds: "Go, sell what you own, and give the money to the poor, and you will have treasure in heaven; then come, follow me." Jesus invites him to discipleship, an itinerant discipleship without the status, security and wealth to which he is accustomed.

This entails becoming like the children in the previous narrative: dependent, receptive, unable to determine the unfolding of his life.[11] Such renunciation is not a condition for everyone wishing to follow Jesus, but it is necessary for this individual. "The cost of discipleship varies with each individual."[12] "Jesus demand is radical in character. He claims the man utterly and completely, and orders the removal of every other support which could interfere with an unconditional obedience."[13] Taken aback by Jesus' challenge, appalled by what is required, he sadly turns away in shock and disappointment, and walks away into the distance, "for he had many possessions." His is "the saddest story in the gospel, this refusal of one whom Jesus loved to follow him."[14] Jesus then comments to his disciples about the difficulty for those with riches to enter the Kingdom of God.

Reflections

Before reflecting on the implications of the story for young people, we need to let the story address ourselves. As Christians, we have accepted the invitation of Jesus to follow him. Perhaps we have not felt asked like the young man in the story to sell everything as part of our discipleship, but the fundamental issue and challenge remains. What is it in my life at present that prevents me from making Jesus utterly central? What is it which hinders or even prevents my growth into deeper relationship with him, clearer living of his values, more committed involvement with his mission? Awareness of our own struggles will help us in our educative responsibility and mission with the young.

In today's secularised world, young people, even if basically good and upright, are prone to accept the cultural norm concerning possessions. The advertising companies work so hard, creatively and insidiously to convince them that they must have the best phones, the most up-to-date high-tech equipment, the trendiest footwear and clothes, and so on. The distinction between what I want and what I need easily becomes blurred. Self-absorption can accelerate. It is also difficult for them to avoid adopting the mentality of success, status, independence, etc. It can be a question of what I have that matters, rather than who I am; or who I am becomes determined by what I have. Jesus, of course, would challenge this. And as parents, educators, pastors or friends, it is our task to help young people to see the alternative view. And words are not enough; they must see it in our own attitudes and lifestyle.[15]

Jesus also points the young man in the story to a realisation of the needs of the poor and to his responsibility for helping them. In our wider world and in our own towns and cities, there is so much hunger and poverty. When they become aware of this, young people usually respond with generosity and ingenuity. This we need to foster and support. In the story, Jesus shows his love for the young man by challenging him. He clearly wants the best for him, "life in all its fullness" (John 10:10). And a significant aspect of accompanying the young is to know when and how to challenge. It needs to be done in a context of affection and care, and in a way which does not come across as judgemental but is positive and liberating.

Finally, I believe the fundamental question of discipleship is raised here, and the issue of vocation in the wide sense of the term. We must find ways of helping young people to face these crucial life issues with openness, realism, courage and freedom. What is God asking of them in life, and offering to them? What is life really about? A deep relationship with Jesus is such a wonderful option; it is a friendship which can enable one's potential to reach fulfilment in ways beyond our expectations. All are called to this, for it is the core of Christian living. Young people need help to discern their own particular call, their personal and unique way of living out this relationship initiated in baptism. Are they called to marriage and family life, to committed single life, religious life, priesthood, missionary outreach, volunteering or other forms of ministry? Work and forms of professional life are also deeply vocational. Young people need adults who can really listen to them, and understand, mentor and accompany them.[16]

This Gospel story, as presented by Mark, is really about the love of Jesus. All the demands made of us in discipleship stem from his love for us, and his desire that our potential, which he can clearly see, can be fully realised.[17] We can easily lose sight of this. We are called to accompany young people in this journey of friendship with Jesus, a journey which we ourselves have embarked upon, and are following through.[18]

Endnotes

1   This suggests that he is a religious authority, perhaps involved in synagogue leadership. I have reflected on Luke's version in *Walking with Luke*, 120–127.

2   Like the leper in 1:40. Culpepper, *Mark*, 334, considers it extravagant that he should run, kneel, and address Jesus as "good teacher".

3   For instance, Nineham, *Mark*, 270, comments: "The stranger was altogether too obsequious and effusive in his approach." On the other hand, Moloney, *Mark*, 198, refers to "sincere enthusiasm". Hooker, *Mark*, 241, is also more positive.

4   Donahue & Harrington, *Mark*, 302, see "eternal life" as synonymous for the Kingdom of God; Boring, *Mark*, 294, for eschatological salvation; Hooker, *Mark*, 241; Moloney, *Mark*, 198, n. 141. The phrase "inherit eternal life" is common in Jewish writings of the time. According to Moloney, *Mark*, 200, n. 150, "treasure in heaven" does not refer to the afterlife; it is a typical Jewish circumlocution avoiding the name of God; his treasure will be with God rather than with himself.

5   Nineham, *Mark*, 270, observes that most Jews would have taken it for granted that keeping the Law was enough, and so would not have asked the question.

6   Matthew (19:17) changes the wording, for Jesus says: "Why do you ask me about what is good? There is only one who is good."

7   Boring, *Mark*, 294, observes that the issue here is the sovereignty of God; the terms of admission to the Kingdom remain God's prerogative.

8   Boring, *Mark*, 295, suggests that Mark may be signalling that the rich man, though personally moral, understands ethics in personal, individualistic terms and is oblivious to his involvement in corporate guilt, economic exploitation. Culpepper, *Mark*, 336, suggests that because the man was rich, he was more likely to have defrauded than to have coveted; or covetousness may lead to defrauding. Also, Moloney, *Mark*, 199. At this point Matthew adds "You shall love your neighbour as yourself."

9   Martin, *Mark*, 259, believes that this indicates that he is no longer a youth. Matthew thinks differently, and by our current standards Matthew may indeed be correct. A Jewish boy took on these responsibilities at the age of 13.

10   This is the only time that Mark states that Jesus loved someone. McBride, *Mark*, 160, comments that Jesus' reaction is one of graciousness and tenderness. Anderson, *Mark*, 249, suggests that Jesus openly showed his affection by putting his arms round him, or had profound sympathy for him in his need. Culpepper, *Mark*, 336, notes that Jesus' radical demand is not a test, but flows from his love for him.

11   Boring, *Mark*, 295. Donahue & Harrington, *Mark*, 304, note that as a rich man he could be a benefactor, which would enhance his reputation. In divesting himself of his goods, he would be deprived of that role too. Culpepper, *Mark*, 337, observes that this is the only time in Mark that Jesus tells a would-be disciple to sell everything and give to the poor. This is a stronger theme in Luke.

12   McBride, *Mark*, 161.

13   Lane, *Mark*, 368.

14   Harrington, *Mark*, 158. Carroll, *Luke*, 364, n. 131; Johnson, *Luke*, 277; George B. Caird, *St. Luke* (London: Pelican, 1963), 205. Green, *Luke*, 656, makes the point that Jesus is not primarily advocating an asceticism of renunciation; the disposition of property is for the sake of the poor, thus following a biblical concern, participating in Jesus' ministry to the poor, rejecting concerns of status honour, and denoting identification with Jesus himself.

15   Pope Francis, *Christus Vivit,* 36, writes: "As members of the Church…we must dare to be different, to point to ideals other than those of this world, testifying to the beauty of generosity, service, purity, perseverance, forgiveness, fidelity to our personal vocation, prayer, the pursuit of justice and the common good, love for the poor, and social friendship."

16   In *Christus Vivit,* 242–247, Pope Francis deals with the issue of accompaniment. He devotes the whole of chapter 8 to the theme of vocation. See also Louis Grech, *Accompanying Youth in a Quest for Meaning* (Bolton: Don Bosco Publications, 2019); Rosanno Sala, *A Guidebook for Salesian Young People and Those who Work with Them* (Bolton: Don Bosco Publications, 2020), 29–41.

17   Pope Francis, *Christus Vivit,* 17–18, reflects on this story. He comments that the young man demonstrates "that youthful openness of spirit which seeks new horizons and great challenges." He wanted something more, but when challenged, he was not able to let go of everything. Later in his Exhortation, Pope Francis urges young people to follow their hopes and dreams, to avoid giving up and anxiety, to take risks, to make the most of the present moment (146–149). He then has a beautiful section on our friendship with Jesus (150–157). The Pope speaks of a dream whose name is Jesus, planted by the Father in the confidence that it would grow and live in every heart. A concrete dream who is a person, running through our veins, thrilling our hearts and making them dance. The whole of chapter eight is devoted to the theme of vocation in its various forms, and chapter nine concentrates on discernment.

18   John calls this relationship "Abiding"; see my *Salesian Gospel Spirituality,* 39–61.

Chapter Nine

Jerusalem Children

According to Matthew's story of Jesus, Jesus and his disciples have for some time been heading for Jerusalem, the climax of his ministry. As the group leaves Jericho for the final fifteen-mile ascent of their hundred-mile journey to the capital, Jesus heals two unnamed blind men, who are sitting by the side of the road on the pilgrim route.[1] Matthew emphasises the compassion of Jesus in responding to their cry: "Lord, have mercy on us, Son of David." Moved with compassion, he touches their eyes and restores their sight. The two then follow him on his way, the way to Jerusalem, the way of discipleship.

For Matthew this is the first time that Jesus has visited Jerusalem.[2] It is a dramatic moment in the Gospel's unfolding, and there is a sense of both expectation and foreboding. Jerusalem had been a capital city for a thousand years. Its temple was the focal point of the Jewish world. It was the place where God was present, the place of forgiveness and blessing, the centre of devotion. Some of the most beautiful psalms express the yearning and hopes and joy of the pilgrims as they make the long ascent to Zion.[3] It is estimated that at times of pilgrimage, the population of Jerusalem increased from about 40,000 to as many as 200,000.

Yet Jerusalem and its temple had another face. Rome conquered the land in 63 BCE, and following their normal imperial practice, they used the high priest and priestly and lay aristocracy of Jerusalem, based in the temple, to lead the local administration. Because of power struggles amongst them, Rome appointed Herod, known as the Great, as their puppet ruler. Herod rebuilt the temple on a grand and splendid scale, erected a luxurious palace for himself in the city, established his own aristocratic elite, and built the city of Caesarea Maritima on the coast. At his death in 4 BCE, Rome divided the territory into three parts, and replaced him with three nominees. Archelaus had responsibility for Jerusalem and Judea for several years before being removed from office. Thereafter, Rome exercised its rule through governors, assigning to the priests and aristocracy of Jerusalem the task of managing the practical, day-to-day administration of the city and territory. The temple again became the most important political and economic centre of the country, whilst maintaining its religious influence. But it was now also the centre of Jewish collaboration with Rome, responsible for the keeping of order and the paying of tribute. The resulting Jewish domination system under the hegemony of pagan Rome was oppressive and exploitative. The wealthy and landed elite minority prospered, whilst the condition of the peasants was becoming increasingly onerous.[4] A change was needed and passionately wanted.

It is the beginning of Passover week, a feast traditionally brimming with fervour, hope and longing for liberation. After leaving Jericho, Jesus and his disciples reach the small village of Bethphage, which is probably situated on the ascent of the Mount of Olives, a ridge which lies across the Kedron valley to the east of Jerusalem, parallel to the city wall.[5] Jesus sends two disciples into the village, telling them what to do and what to say. There is a clear note of authority about his instructions. He is aware of what will take place. They will find a donkey and a colt and are to bring them to him. If anyone comments or objects, they are to tell them that "The Lord needs them." This is the only occasion in Matthew when Jesus refers to himself as "Lord". Something of the majesty and glory of Jesus is touching the narrative. His instructions show that his entering the city on a donkey is a deliberate, planned, symbolic act, a prophetic gesture.[6] It fulfils the words of the prophet: "Tell the daughter of Zion, 'Look, your king is coming to you, humble, and mounted on a donkey, and on a colt, the foal of a donkey.'"

It is interesting that Matthew mentions two animals, whereas the other three evangelists refer to one only. Probably the reason for this is to be found in this scriptural quotation from Zechariah which Matthew includes in his narrative, and which refers to "a donkey and a colt, the foal of a donkey."[7] This aspect of the fulfilment quotation is taken literally, even though the original was an example of the typical form of parallelism found in Hebrew poetry, whereby the same thing is described twice in different words. Here the second line makes the meaning of the first more specific.[8] The opening phrase of the scriptural quotation which Matthew has inserted is actually taken from Isaiah: "Say to daughter Zion, 'See, your salvation comes'" (Isa 62:11 LXX). The whole text highlights to the people of Jerusalem that it is their messianic prophet-king who is coming and who takes possession of his city. He makes his solemn entry, however, not on a sleek charger as a military, nationalistic liberator, but in humility on a donkey as a man of gentleness and peace. Surprisingly, Matthew has omitted from the quotation two words which are central to his understanding of Jesus as Messiah, namely "righteous" and "saving".[9] This places all the emphasis on his meekness and humility. Jesus has no military ambitions, no intention of overthrowing the Romans and setting up a national, political kingdom; he is a messiah of a different kind from that which many expected and hoped for.

The disciples go and do as Jesus has instructed, returning with the two animals. There is no mention of their being questioned, as in Mark and Luke. The disciples place their cloaks on the back of the animals to form a saddle, and Jesus mounts. Presumably he mounted one animal, not both, though the text is in the plural, since Matthew wishes to show perfect fulfilment of the prophecy! Jesus does not enter the city on foot, like the other pilgrims; he sits, as does a king. A very large crowd is present, pilgrims going up for the feast. Some spread their cloaks on the road, while others cut branches from the trees in the vicinity and place them on the road ahead of Jesus like a carpet. These are gestures of homage.[10] In this version of the event, there is no mention of palms, which did not grow in the area of Jerusalem.[11] A procession forms, and the pilgrims begin to chant "Hosanna", which means "Save us, we beseech you." By the time of Jesus it had probably lost its original meaning and become a cry of praise and welcome.[12] The crowd recognise the implicit messianic claim of his riding on a donkey and acknowledge Jesus as the "Son of David", and as "the one who comes in the name of the Lord". Matthew understands the title "Son of David" as messianic.[13] He introduces Jesus in the first verse of his Gospel in this way. During the ministry he applies it to Jesus when he is healing afflicted people.[14] The second phrase, an acclamation of praise, comes from Psalm 117:26 (LXX).[15] The original can be taken as "Blessed in the name of the Lord is he who comes", or, as here, as "Blessed is he who comes in the name of the Lord", a messianic acclamation. Jesus comes to his city, indeed, in the name of the Lord.

Jesus enters Jerusalem in triumph as prophetic king, and the whole city is said to be in turmoil, shaken to its foundations. The verb is strong, and is often applied to an earthquake.[16] This recalls the reaction at the outset of the Gospel when the whole of Jerusalem shared Herod's fright and consternation at the arrival of the Magi searching for the newborn King of the Jews (2:3). Again, there is no enthusiastic welcome from the citizens of Jerusalem, simply a wondering question: "Who is this?" The pilgrim crowd responds that it is "Jesus, the prophet from Nazareth in Galilee", which is something of an understatement. The local inhabitants do not realise that their king has arrived, and that the prophecies have been fulfilled.[17]

It is quite probable that at the same time as Jesus was entering the city on a donkey from the East, accompanied by peasant pilgrims, Pilate, the Roman governor, was entering from the West, with his cavalry and soldiers.[18] His base was on the coast, but for major Jewish festivals like Passover he was wont to take up residence himself in Herod's palace, whilst his troops reinforced the garrison stationed in the Fortress of Antonia, overlooking the temple, lest there be trouble. The contrast is striking and profoundly meaningful and prophetic.

The action of the narrative continues as Jesus immediately moves into the temple. In the large court of the Gentiles he drives out those who are buying and selling; he overturns the table of the money changers and the seats of those who sold doves. These activities were central to the sacrificial system of the temple.[19] He states: "My house shall be called a house of prayer; but you are making it a den of robbers."[20] "The action upholds the sanctity of the temple whilst at the same time pointing prophetically to its destruction."[21]

The text which refers to young people follows:

> The blind and the lame came to him in the temple, and he cured them. But when the chief priests and the scribes saw the amazing things that he did, and heard the children crying out in the temple, 'Hosanna to the Son of David', they became angry and said to him, 'Do you hear what these are saying?' Jesus said to them, 'Yes; have you never read, "Out of the mouths of infants and nursing babies you have prepared praise for yourself"?' He left them, went out of the city to Bethany, and spent the night there. (21:14–17)

After Jesus' dramatic prophetic gesture and strongly critical words, there is a change of tone and mood as he reaches out in compassion, as has been his wont throughout his ministry, to heal the lame and blind who come to seek him out in the temple precincts. People like this should not have been in the temple, since their presence was considered incompatible with its holiness (Lev 21:16–24; 2 Sam 5:6–8 LXX).[22] His miracles have always been signs of the presence of the Kingdom; now, for the first and only time, Jesus brings healing within Jerusalem and in the temple itself. The temple, a place of prayer, is a place of wholeness and new life. In the background is heard the shouting of children "Hosanna to the Son of David", echoing the earlier greetings of the crowd as he approached the city earlier that day, and recognising his identity as Davidic messiah.[23] Now that greeting and that recognition of his Davidic messiahship resounds within the temple itself.

On seeing what he was doing in restoring the blind and lame to wholeness, and on hearing the chants of the children, the chief priests and scribes, a formidable pairing, become angry, and protest: "Do you hear what these are saying?"[24] They believe that Jesus should have prevented them or denied their affirmations. They themselves certainly do not accept the truth of the children's acclamation. They are unwilling to recognise the presence of God's reign in Jesus; they do not welcome him to the temple. This is the first of several altercations which will punctuate the next few days. Jesus replies to their indignant comment by quoting Psalm 8:2, a familiar psalm which they ought to have known: "Out of the mouths of infants and nursing babies you have prepared praise for yourself."[25] What the children were saying was true, whether they understood it or not.[26] And God has chosen children to proclaim the truth about the Son.

Jesus then leaves the city after a very eventful day and spends the night in Bethany. Conflict with the religious leaders will resume the following day, as the story of Jesus moves inexorably to its climax.

Reflections

The contrasts in the events of this day are striking. The enthusiasm of disciples and pilgrims is not matched by the Jerusalemites, who are confused and troubled. The joy of the chanting children finds no echo in the antagonism of the religious elite. The style of Jesus' kingship, as he enters his city on a donkey, is so different from Roman power and pomp. The temple is a place which he clears of merchants, and a place where he compassionately brings healing to the suffering. This is also a story of significant prophetic gestures, at the city gate and in the temple. This day sets the scene for the culmination of Jesus' life and ministry. The options of acceptance or rejection are highlighted. And these are options which we cannot avoid ourselves. What do *we* believe about the identity of Jesus? How welcome do *we* make him in our daily lives? Have *we* made our own his style of gentleness and humility, coupled with his outreach to the needy?

And in the story, children once more have an important role. In the very heart of Judaism, the temple, they, the "little ones" are chosen by God, again paradoxically, to acclaim loudly in that sacred place Jesus' identity as Davidic Messiah. Jesus accepts their joyful praise. But their chanting also serves to trigger open conflict, exposing the enemies of Jesus, who are blind and hardened in their opposition to the prophet from Nazareth, and whose determination to be rid of him is sharpened.

Again, we are reminded that God speaks to us often through the young. Frequently, they have a keener perception than adults, they can highlight the essential, identify genuineness in people and situations. It is so important that we listen and do not dismiss their views and ideas, not least in matters which pertain to liturgy and Church. Young people need to know that they are welcome and accepted and part of the worshipping community. This was the purpose of the Synod. We adults need to be aware of our own preconceptions and prejudices, and be open to be disturbed, challenged and, perhaps, to change.[27]

There is possibly a further lesson from this text. The temple is "a house of prayer", but for Jesus it is also a house of healing and compassionate care for the suffering. For us, too, our prayer cannot be separated from outreach to others, especially those in need. We cannot expect God to respond to the needs we place before him in prayer if we are unwilling to respond to the needs of our brothers and sisters.[28]

Endnotes

1 Matt 20:29-34. In Mark there is one man only, named Bartimaeus.

2 This is true also for Mark and Luke. In John, Jesus makes several visits and spends time there.

3 Psalms 120-134.

4 See Marcus J. Borg and John Dominic Crossan, *The Last Week* (London: SPCK, 2008), 1-30.

5 Zechariah 14:4 states that the Mount of Olives will be the place where the final struggle will happen on the Day of the Lord. Jesus pronounces his eschatological discourse from there in 24:3ff. Bethphage means 'house of unripe figs', and technically lay within the city boundary.

6 The donkey or ass was used in royal ceremonies in the Ancient Near East and also in Judea. Solomon rode David's royal donkey when going to be anointed king (2 Sam 18:9; 19:26; 1 Kings 1:31-32). Davies & Allison, *Matthew*, 344, state that rabbinic literature makes the donkey a messianic animal.

7 Zechariah 9:9 (MT). Formula quotations of this kind are a characteristic feature of Matthew's Gospel. Hagner, *Matthew*, 2:594, notes that an unbroken colt was usually introduced into service accompanied by its parent. He considers it probable that historically two animals were involved. Davies & Allison, *Matthew*, 345, observe that "Say to the daughter of Zion" (the people of Jerusalem) makes it plain that the entrance and acclamation demand a response from Jerusalem.

8   Senior, *Matthew*, 230, maintains that this is the kind of literal exactness not uncommon in Jewish interplay with biblical allusions. Meier, *Matthew*, 232, suggests that Matthew is more interested in literal fulfilment than historical probability. Davies & Allison, *Matthew*, 346, refer to Exod 4:19–20 and Moses traditions.

9   Or "triumphant and victorious" (9:9b).

10   Luz, *Matthew*, 3:9.

11   The palm tradition comes from John's version (12:13). Palms were associated with Maccabean nationalism. They appear on coins minted from 140BCE to 70CE, with the words "for the liberation of Israel." See Moloney, *John*, 360; Lincoln, *John*, 343.

12   Meier, *Matthew*, 233; Hagner, *Matthew*, 2:595.

13   See Senior, *Matthew*, 230.

14   See 9:27; 12:23; 15:22; 20:30; 21:15

15   Psalm 118 in the MT.

16   Byrne, *Lifting the Burden*, 158, n.5. See 8:24; 24:7; 27:51–54; 28:2–4.

17   Davies & Allison, *Matthew*, 349, note the irony and pathos of the passage. The "daughter of Zion" does not understand. The acclamation of Jesus does not come from those within the city. Luz, *Matthew*, 3:10, describes the situation well: these verses "intimate the coming division in Israel. On the one side are the shaken Jerusalemites, in fear because of the arrival of the Messiah. On the other side are the crowds who praise Jesus."

18   Borg and Crossan, *Last Week*, 2–3.

19   Greek and Roman coins, which had images which were offensive to the Jews, could be changed into Tyrian and Jewish coins. Senior, *Matthew*, 231, suggests that much of the activity was necessary and was not venal, but Jesus wishes prophetically to purge the temple of all commercial transactions. Meier, *Matthew*, 235, points out that the businesses were controlled by the priestly aristocracy, so Jesus' action could be considered an attack on the priesthood. Hagner, *Matthew*, 2:600, observes that animals for sacrifice were available for purchase at special facilities on the Mount of Olives. Luz, *Matthew*, 3:11, notes that today the temple cleansing is usually interpreted as a prophetic symbolic action. However, only a relatively obscure event would explain why neither the temple police not the Roman garrison intervened. Beare, *Matthew*, 415–416, highlights the large number of animals and pigeons for sacrifice, and their attendants and merchants, the problems for the pilgrims; he believes that a large-scale event is implausible.

20   The composite quotation comes from Isa 56:7 ("house of prayer") and Jer 7:11 ("den of robbers"). Davies & Allison, *Matthew*, 350, comment that Jesus, as prophet, declared God's disfavour, which is not directed against the temple as such, but against those who have corrupted the institution, preventing the temple from being what God intended it to be, a house of prayer. Luz, *Matthew*, 3:11–12, suggests three possible interpretations: Jesus' action indicates the restoration of the true cult or the holiness of the entire temple; the destruction of the present temple; or is directed against the economic power of the temple aristocracy that misused

the temple by carrying on business to make a profit, not least the sellers of doves, who create difficulties for the poor. He feels the arguments for the third view are strongest, though it may be possible to combine it with the other views. H.B. Green, *Matthew*, 176, believes Jesus' action can be seen both as a prophet's symbolic action and as a pointed challenge to those who had responsibility for the temple.

21   Byrne, *Lifting the Burden*, 159; Senior, *Matthew*, 232. For a detailed discussion of this episode in Jesus' life, see Nicholas Perrin, *Jesus the Temple* (London: SPCK, 2010), 80–113. He sees Jesus' action as, first, a sign against the temple because of the corruption, greed and financial irregularities of the temple leadership, which had a deleterious effect on the poor, and, secondly, as a messianic claim to be the builder of the new eschatological temple.

22   Luz, *Matthew*, 3:13, offers a different view, believing that their presence was normal; also, Bartholomé, *Los Niños*, 204.

23   Hagner, *Matthew*, 2:602, suggests the children in all good fun were mimicking the chant they had heard earlier.

24   The priests have responsibility for the temple; the scribes have been hostile to Jesus before (16:21; 20:18). It is perhaps surprising that they do not express concern about Jesus' prophetic action in the temple.

25   The Greek term used for the children who call out is *paides*; in the quotation from the Psalm the two words are *nēpioi* and *thēlazontes*. The different response of the children and the religious elite recall the words of Jesus in his earlier prayer (11:25); also 19:13–15. The rest of that verse in the psalm is omitted: "to silence the enemy and the avenger." Jewish exegesis linked the psalm with Moses and Exodus (15:2). The children in the temple are not infants, as in the psalm; they are old enough to go to the temple alone. In Luke 19:38–40, as Jesus and his disciples and the crowds enter Jerusalem, the Pharisees demand that he should stop his disciples from proclaiming him as the king who is coming in the name of the Lord. Jesus replies: "I tell you, if these were silent, the stones would shout out." Davies & Allison, *Matthew*, 352, comment that the identity of the children and the temple setting serve to confirm God's approval of Jesus.

26   Hagner, *Matthew*, 2:602.

27   Pope Francis, *Christus Vivit*, 38, notes that "We need to make more room for the voices of young people to be heard." In 37, he states that the young can stop the Church from becoming corrupt, prevent her from being proud and sectarian, help her to be poorer and to bear better witness, to fight for justice and let herself be challenged.

28   Bartholomé, *Los Niños*, 210.

CHAPTER TEN

The Markan Ending

Mark's story of Jesus has been gradually but clearly moving to its Calvary climax. His Passion Narrative is excellently crafted, beginning with the Passover meal. The structure of the meal is powerful.[1] With simplicity and economy[2] it contains three episodes, two at the Supper itself, and a third as Jesus and his disciples leave the supper room for the Mount of Olives. First, Jesus speaks about the coming betrayal to be perpetrated by one of the Twelve, a friend and table companion, who partakes of the same dish (14:17-21; see Ps 41:9).[3] Secondly, he then speaks words over the bread and cup; this is Mark's main focus (14:22-25). And thirdly, as they leave the supper room after the meal and concluding psalms, Jesus, in shepherding language recalling Zechariah (13:7), foretells the scattering and flight of all the disciples and the denials of Peter (14:26-31). But in the tragedy of it all there is a note of hope as he promises that he will later go before them into Galilee. The two pointers to the inadequacy and failure of the disciples, his close friends, chosen to be "with him" (3:14), serve as the framework for the words and action of Jesus, which express his deep self-giving love. This structural shape highlights the significance of the central event and the contrast between Jesus and his disciples. It also shows that Mark's agenda, as throughout his Gospel, includes both the self-giving of Jesus and the failure of his disciples.[4]

The disciples have accompanied Jesus from the supper room, across the Kidron ravine, and into Gethsemane, where Jesus has prayed to the Father. Returning for the third time to the disciples, Jesus says: "The hour has come;

the Son of Man is betrayed into the hands of sinners. Get up, let us be going. See, my betrayer is at hand." Then:

> Immediately, while he was still speaking, Judas, one of the twelve, arrived; and with him there was a crowd with swords and clubs, from the chief priests, the scribes, and the elders. Now the betrayer had given them a sign, saying, 'The one I will kiss is the man; arrest him and lead him away under guard.' So when he came, he went up to him at once and said, 'Rabbi!' and kissed him. Then they laid hands on him and arrested him. But one of those who stood near drew his sword and struck the slave of the high priest, cutting off his ear. Then Jesus said to them, 'Have you come out with swords and clubs to arrest me as though I were a bandit? Day after day I was with you in the temple teaching, and you did not arrest me. But let the scriptures be fulfilled.' All of them deserted him and fled.
>
> A certain young man was following him, wearing nothing but a linen cloth. They caught hold of him, but he left the linen cloth and ran off naked. (14: 43–52)

At this dramatic and crucial moment, we find mention of a young man (*neaniskos*), who was "following him", the key Markan term for discipleship. It is a strange, puzzling and enigmatic episode. The eleven followers long associated with Jesus (3:13–19), lose no time in taking to their heels, as predicted, leaving Jesus to face his fate alone. The youth was not quite so quick, and members of the arresting party, having seized Jesus, now catch hold of him. Clearly, they consider him to be "one of them". But he manages to slip away, leaving his garment in their hands, disappearing naked into the darkness (like Joseph in Gen 39:12). He joins the other disciples in flight. Mark is the only evangelist to record this episode. There is no indication who the young man is, where he comes from, or how he has got into this situation. Like the others, his own safety becomes his priority.

Some scholars, taking the story as factual, have speculated that he is James, the Lord's brother; others suggest he could be the evangelist himself, adroitly including himself in the narrative.[5] His real identity will probably always remain elusive. "He stands for those who desert Jesus in times of trouble."[6] Moloney calls it "a parabolic story" or commentary, in which the young man is a model of the disciples as a group.[7] In biblical thinking nakedness is a sign of shame (see Amos 2:16). So, he opts for shame rather than fidelity to Jesus.[8] The word translated "linen cloth" (*sindōn*) is also used of the burial cloth of Jesus; it was usually made from fine linen and was an expensive item. "In abandoning his clothing, the young man had abandoned not only Jesus, but the new identity he had received as a follower of Jesus."[9] Like the others, having left everything to follow Jesus, he now ignominiously leaves everything not to do so.¹⁰ Earlier, Jesus explained the nature of discipleship as being prepared to lose one's life for his sake (8:34–35). Here, failure wins the day.

Mark's presentation of the passion and death of Jesus is a powerful piece of writing. One of its main theological themes is the aloneness or isolation of Jesus, as he is betrayed by one of his closest followers, abandoned by all the others in the garden of arrest, and later denied with a curse by his main disciple, Simon Peter. The religious leaders of his nation unanimously find him guilty and deserving of death, the Jerusalem populace opt for the release of Jesus Barabbas, the murderer, rather than Jesus of Nazareth, and shout that he should be handed over to the hideous torture death of crucifixion. On the cross he is mocked by ordinary passers-by, soldiery and scribes, and even the two crucified with him disown him. There is no mother or beloved disciple on Calvary, and the women who are present stand at a distance. The searing anguish of his pain, loneliness and failure is focused and captured in the loud cry from the cross: "My God, my God, why hast thou forsaken me?" He dies utterly alone.¹¹ After the death of the Baptist in Herod's prison, his disciples came, took away his body and buried it in a tomb.¹² In the case of Jesus this service is performed by a stranger, a non-Galilean Sanhedrin member, a pious, observant Jew "waiting expectantly for the kingdom of God," the fulfilment of God's promises.¹³

But that is not the end of the story of Jesus, nor of the disciples. For:

> When the sabbath was over, Mary Magdalene, and Mary the mother of James, and Salome bought spices, so that they might go and anoint him. And very early on the first day of the week, when the sun had risen, they went to the tomb. They had been saying to one another, 'Who will roll away the stone for us from the entrance to the tomb?' When they looked up, they saw that the stone, which was very large, had already been rolled back. As they entered the tomb, they saw a young man, dressed in a white robe, sitting on the right side; and they were alarmed. But he said to them, 'Do not be alarmed; you are looking for Jesus of Nazareth, who was crucified. He has been raised; he is not here. Look, there is the place they laid him. But go, tell his disciples and Peter that he is going ahead of you to Galilee; there you will see him, just as he told you.' So they went out and fled from the tomb, for terror and amazement had seized them; and they said nothing to anyone, for they were afraid. (16:1–8)

With his introductory phrase "When the Sabbath was over", Mark resumes his narrative after the silence of the Sabbath rest, and links the Easter story with his description of the death and the subsequent burial of Jesus.¹⁴ The women are named as Mary Magdalene, Mary the mother of James, and Salome. They were present on Calvary, "looking on from a distance".¹⁵ Not having obtained spices on Friday, and having observed the Sabbath faithfully, the women go on Saturday evening to buy some, presumably with a view to using them next morning. Early on that Sunday morning, "the first day of the week", after the rising of the sun, a symbolic comment, they make the journey to the tomb in which Jesus was buried. Its location they know because of their presence at the burial. Because of the hurried nature of Jesus' burial, and also because it was 'dishonourable', their intention seems to be to rectify the omission. Presumably, they were also motivated by grief and loving devotion; perhaps they also sought some sort of closure. It was not unusual in that culture for relatives to visit the grave for three days after burial; in fact, mourning was at its height on the third day. Perhaps it was unrealistic of the women in such a climate to think of anointing a corpse after three days, but love and concern often override practical considerations. From their actions it is clear that they are concerned about a corpse; the possibility of Jesus' resurrection has never entered their heads.

Whilst on the way, the women wonder how they will manage to roll the stone away from the tomb entrance, given its size. As a good storyteller, Mark is creating dramatic tension and excitement, preparing for the amazing and totally unexpected surprise which follows. For, on arriving, they find the tomb open, the large stone already rolled away. The passive verb indicates the action of God; the women look up and "see" what God has done.

Having moved inside the tomb, the women find, not the body of Jesus, but "a young man" (*neaniskos*) in a white robe, the traditional attire of heavenly beings; he is seated on the right hand side, the position of an authoritative teacher. This figure is undoubtedly an interpreting angel, a messenger from God.[16] This is the way Matthew and Luke interpret Mark. It was quite typical in the Old Testament to describe an appearing angel as a young man and describe heavenly beings as clothed in white (2 Macc 3:26, 33; 5:2; Tob 5:9). Some scholars make a link with the young man of the garden scene, who left his "linen cloth" in the hands of members of the arresting party, and abandoned Jesus in flight.[17] The clothing now is different, and the "linen cloth" in which the body of Jesus was wrapped is no longer in the tomb. In the garden the "young man" was a symbol of the failed disciples; now his presence is a hint of God's power to reverse the failure of the disciples too; they also have a future.[18] The main point of Mark's story is that God's messenger announces the resurrection to the women. The women are overcome with amazement and fear at this unexpected occurrence; the verb indicates intense feelings of awe at the numinous, the reaction which normally accompanies heavenly manifestations. After seeking to dispel the women's fear, the role of the angelic youth is to proclaim the Easter message: "Do not be alarmed; you are looking for Jesus of Nazareth, who was crucified. He has been raised; he is not here. Look, there is the place they laid him."

The death of Jesus is not the end of his story. "He has been raised; he is not here". His faithful God and Father has not forsaken him, but has vindicated him, as Jesus had foretold, dramatically reversing his apparent failure, and conquering death. Jesus is named as "Jesus of Nazareth" (the "Nazarene", *ton Nazarēnon*), as at the outset of Mark's narrative.[19] In this way the evangelist draws together his entire story, and indicates that "the Jesus whom God has raised from the dead is no other Jesus than the one with whom he began his story, namely the Jesus who is God's beloved Son."[20] The startling antithesis and contrast between "was crucified", and "was raised" by God is typical of the kerygmatic formulas and faith confessions of the early Church. The insight of the centurion on Calvary into the true identity of Jesus is confirmed. The formula rings out like a triumphant shout of victory. Through the angel/young man, God proclaims the resurrection of the Son. After the proclamation comes a reference to the tomb, the place where "they" had laid him, and now the reason for its emptiness becomes evident.

The focus now switches to the disciples. "As God transformed the death of Jesus by raising him from the dead, discipleship may be re-established and nakedness covered."[21] The women are sent on mission to the disciples, leaving the empty tomb behind. In spite of their failure and flight, their choice not to "be with" him, their unwillingness to accept the shame of belonging to him, they are still considered to be his disciples. In spite of his threefold denial, his emphatically sworn choice no longer to "be with" Jesus, Peter is still singled out for special mention. The risen Lord remains faithful; he has forgiven them, and he calls them back to him once more in Galilee, as promised (14:28), where it had all begun, where they had been with him, been taught by him, witnessed his mighty deeds, and had experienced mission. There they will "see" him. "The blindness that characterised the disciples throughout (see 8:18) will be lifted, to be replaced by seeing the risen Jesus in Galilee."[22]

Mark's story ends on a puzzling note: "So they went out and fled from the tomb, for terror and amazement had seized them; and they said nothing to anyone, for they were afraid."

The women, who had remained true and stood by Jesus when all the men failed, are now overcome by fear and astonishment, terror and consternation, and they, too, take flight. Their fear is connected with the appearance and message of the "young man". In the face of God's action, a reaction of fear is not unnatural and is a common biblical feature. They are unable to cope with the experience and the news. Their ongoing silence, expressed in a double negative, is, however, more problematic.

Mark and his community were obviously aware that Jesus had, as promised, appeared to his followers, and that the Church was already spreading far and wide. They were a living part of that Church. The issue is why Mark chose to end his story of Jesus abruptly in this way.[23] Many scholarly explanations have been put forward. A frequently adduced view is that perhaps Mark is seeking to underline the mystery, wonder, awesomeness and supernatural character of resurrection.[24] Perhaps he wishes to emphasise our human inadequacy in the face of God's action. Maybe he wanted God to have the last word, the God who bestows the gift of Easter faith.[25] "Throughout the gospel men and women have been blind and deaf to the truth about Jesus, and now at the end, when the divine message is delivered to the women, they are struck dumb, and fail to deliver it."[26] It is Mark's final irony. The verse with which the Gospel ends "drives home with considerable force the women's sharing in one of the fundamental aspects of the disciples' failure to follow Jesus to the cross: fear (4:41; 6:50; 9:32; 10:32)."[27] The women join the other disciples in their failure. Mark takes all initiative away from human beings, for they all fail; he places it with the overspilling goodness, incredible faithfulness, and gratuitous love of God.[28] It is the Father's transforming action which has vindicated the Son's generous and loving self-gift in death. And it is the Father's action which has transformed the fearful and failed disciples and brought the Christian community into existence. God is centre stage. Mark's story challenges us, centuries later, to accept Jesus' way, and in our struggles and failures assures us of God's ongoing faithfulness, trustworthiness, and transforming power. By ending as he does, the masterstroke of a storyteller,[29] Mark "leaves his readers, who may have thought that the story was about somebody else, with a decision to make... "[30]

Reflections

In some ways, the ending of Mark's Gospel is bleak. Both women and men fail; they are indeed "fallible followers", to use Malbon's terminology.[31] We admit that we probably find ourselves in their company. Failure and fear are part of our experience, too, centuries later. In fact, the number of times that key figures in the Bible are instructed by God not to be afraid illustrates the pervasive nature of fear. No other command or exhortation is more frequently made. Fear can hold us back from surrendering to God and God's involving us in His saving plan. Perhaps it is the fear of losing ourselves, of losing control over our lives; maybe it is the fear of being found wanting, of being inadequate. Fear can often prevent us from reaching out to others; it can be an obstacle to friendship and intimacy, to community and collaboration, to service and self-giving; fear can make it extremely difficult to trust others. Fear can stifle compassion, thwart growth, deaden dreams, cramp initiative, crush potential, sap life energy. Fear can severely hinder genuine discernment. So much of the violence and aggression within us and around us in our country and our wider world is born of fear and is sustained and fuelled by it. We can be afraid of challenge, of failure, of being marginalised, of becoming useless. We can be afraid of what others may think or say. We can be afraid of suffering and of death. Fear can also prevent us from reaching out to young people, responding to their needs, facing their challenges.

We can, however, take heart, for the God behind Mark's story and our story is always faithful. And the Jesus He calls his "Son, the Beloved", is faithful too. Throughout the breathless narrative subsequent to his initial lakeside encounter with the two pairs of fishermen, Jesus has remained true to his disciples, despite their fragility, dullness, and capacity to get it wrong, spectacularly at times. Beyond the tragic mess and failure of that final week in Jerusalem, he summons them back to Galilee to start again. In the Old Testament God is understood above all as faithful love. This is the God made known in Jesus. This is how the darkness of Calvary is transformed into the bright dawn of Easter day. This is how our own shadows and darkness and our fears, too, will be transformed, as God's faithful love is revealed in our own life experience as fallible disciples of Jesus.

Like the youth in the garden, young people today can at times fail and let us down, sometimes badly. They can get involved with various projects, and then lose interest. At school, at home, at university, in the parish or youth club, or in finding work, they can make decisions which are painful for us. This can be because they wish to do their own thing, get their own way, be independent. Sometimes their failure can be the result of fear: fear of their peers, for instance. Some reject family and Church, becoming displaced, and even more vulnerable. An important issue for us is how we respond to all this. Mark shows how Jesus responded to the failure of the disciples: forgiveness, faithfulness, sticking with them, not abandoning them, gently welcoming back. And this was because he loved them, and loved them deeply, despite their fragility. Jesus models the response we are called to make, the message that we need to communicate to them. Whatever they do, God loves them still, with a love they cannot lose, and so do we.

Many young people are themselves let down by adults—parents and relatives, teachers and clergy, politicians and leaders. This can erode trust and confidence, can lead to hostility, isolation and independence. It can therefore be extremely destructive. The whole area of safeguarding touches us here. Finding ways of helping and bringing healing is an imperative for us. These young people need to experience genuine affection. I think it is so refreshing that Mark chooses a *'neaniskos'*, a youth, albeit angelic, to reveal the good news of Jesus' resurrection to the women at the tomb. Young people, in different ways and at different ages, can be bearers of good news, can be sources of encouragement, new life, hope and meaning. I know in my community how true that is. Young people bring new ideas, enthusiasm, energy, drive, transformation. They can enable us to rediscover what it can mean to be really alive.[32]

Endnotes

1   See Francis J. Moloney, *A Body Broken for a Broken People. Marriage, Divorce, and the Eucharist* (Mulgrave: Garratt, 2015), 83; he explains and illustrates Mark's literary technique of "framing". The central story of Jesus' meal with his disciples is framed between predictions of Judas' betrayal and later Peter's denials and the future flight of the disciples. We discussed an excellent example of "framing" in Chapter One.

2   Anderson, *Mark, Gospel,* 311.

3   Boring, *Mark,* 389, notes that "eating with" in that culture indicates a close relationship; therefore "the new community Jesus has called into being is undergoing an extremely serious crisis."

4   Moloney, *Body Broken,* 84, provides a structural outline for 14:1–72 showing how Mark has created a pattern of alternating scenes reporting the activities of Jesus and the disciples; vv. 17–31, the Supper, is in the centre of this structure. Donahue & Harrington, *Mark,* 399, note the influence of Old Testament motifs in Mark's story, especially Zech 9–14, and Servant texts (Isa 53). Donald Senior, *The Passion of Jesus in the Gospel of Mark* (Wilmington: Glazier, 1984), 54, states that Mark uses this scene as an interpretation of Jesus' entire mission, and of the disciples' stake in it.

5   For a list of the many suggestions which have been made, see McBride, *Mark,* 235; Boring, *Mark,* 403. For Nineham, *Mark,* 396, the endless speculation is profitless. Raymond E. Brown, *The Death of the Messiah,* 2 vols. (London: Geoffrey Chapman, 1994), 1:299, concludes his discussion: "In my judgement these suggestions are nothing other than flights of fancy." Culpepper, *Mark,* 513, notes that this is a reversal of Bartimaeus, who throws aside his cloak to come to Jesus (10:50). Anderson, *Mark,* 324, on the other hand, suggests that the story most

likely rests on historical reminiscence, and is included, perhaps, to draw a contrast between the escaping youth and Jesus, who makes no such attempt. Hooker, *Mark*, 352, refers to the possibility of a historical reminiscence concerning the arrest, interpreted as the fulfilment of scripture.

6   Donahue & Harrington, *Mark*, 417.

7   Moloney, *Mark*, 299.

8   Boring, *Mark*, 403; Donahue & Harrington, *Mark*, 417.

9   Boring, *Mark*, 404. Senior, *Passion*, 84, mentions the view that the incident is a symbolic prelude to the resurrection story: as Jesus is arrested, the narrative flashes ahead to the empty tomb story. Jesus will ultimately escape from the clutches of death in resurrection, shedding his burial garments as the young man does in the garden.

10   Martin, *Mark*, 398. Brown, *Death*, 1:303. Culpepper, *Mark*, 513, considers that he represents the tragic plight of the disciples who left everything to follow Jesus (10:28) and then abandoned him. "His nakedness reflects their shame." Brown, *Death*, 1:303, considers his flight as even more desperate than that of the other disciples. Senior, *Passion*, 85, concludes by saying that while the symbolic meaning or the fact of a historical reminiscence cannot be ruled out, the young man's flight reinforces the impression of a complete breakdown on the part of the disciples. "Their fear totally overwhelms their allegiance to Jesus."

11   See Michael T. Winstanley, *Come and See* (London: DLT, 1985), 100–110; Gerhard Lohfink, *Jesus of Nazareth. What He wanted. Who He was.* Translated by Linda M. Maloney. (Collegeville, MN: Liturgical Press, 2012), 289.

12   6:29

13   See Moloney, *Mark*, 333; Nineham, *Mark*, 434; Hooker, *Mark*, 381; Martin, *Mark*, 444; Brown, *Death*, 2:1216. The phrase can apply to pious observers of the Law. Earlier (14:34) the good scribe is described as being "not far from the kingdom of God". Donahue & Harrington, *Mark*, 456, link him with this scribe in being examples of the best in the religious tradition of Israel. For Luke, Joseph is "a good and righteous man," a Sanhedrin member "who had not agreed with their plan and action". Wright, *Mark*, 220, maintains that he must have been a secret supporter of Jesus, which is the view of John 19:38. For Matthew (27:57) he is "a disciple of Jesus". Byrne, *A Costly Freedom*, 259, suggests that perhaps he was a later convert. In favour of a burial of Jesus by the Jews, see Acts 13:27–29; John 19:31.I have reflected on this passage in *Alive: The Gospel Resurrection Narratives, Then and Now* (Bolton: Don Bosco Publications, 2018), 11–12.

14   It is therefore "the third day" (8:31; 9:31; 10:34; 14:58; 15:29).

15   On Calvary (15:40) the second Mary is said to be the mother of James the younger and Joses; these women "used to follow him and provided for him when he was in Galilee". At the burial (15:47), there is no mention of Salome, and the Mary is named as the mother (or daughter) of Joses. Mark makes no attempt to harmonise his lists. Hooker, *Mark*, 383, suggests that he was probably reproducing different independent traditions; similarly, Culpepper, *Mark*, 584.

16   The interpreting angel is a feature of apocalyptic literature (see Zech 1-6; Dan 7-12; Rev 1:1; 19:9-22:16). See Moloney, *Mark*, 345; W. Harrington, *Mark* (Dublin: Veritas, 1979), 244; McBride, *Mark*, 262; Culpepper, *Mark*, 586; Brown, *Death*, 1:299-300.

17   Moloney, *Mark*, 345-46: "The verbal links are too many, and the passages follow one another too closely within the story to be irrelevant." See Culpepper, *Mark*, 586; W. Harrington, *Mark*, 245; Martin, *Mark*, 450.

18   Boring, *Mark*, 445; Moloney, Mark, 345-46; *The Resurrection of the Messiah*, (New York: Paulist Press, 2013), 10-11.

19   Culpepper, *Mark*, 588, suggests that this detail may imply fulfilment of the promise "of the temple not made with hands"

20   Jack Dean Kingsbury, *The Christology of Mark's Gospel*, (Philadelphia: Fortress, 1983), 153. See Brown, *A Risen Christ in Eastertime* (Collegeville, MI: The Liturgical Press, 1991), 13-14.

21   Moloney, *Mark*, 345; *Resurrection*, 11.

22   Donohue & Harrington, *Mark*, 461.

23   I accept the view of most scholars today that Mark intended his Gospel to end at 16:8, awkward though it is. Some scholars suggest that Mark may have been prevented from including a resurrection appearance by sudden death, or that a final page of the original manuscript was lost or destroyed. For more details see my *Alive*, 18, n. 13; Culpepper, *Mark*, 589-90; Moloney, *Mark*, 340-341.

24   Nineham, *Mark*, 448. Moloney, *Mark*, 349, calls this the traditional solution to the problem.

25   Anderson, *Mark*, 358. Byrne, *A Costly Freedom*, 258, suggests that Mark wishes to emphasise that resurrection faith was not the result of the empty tomb or the women's testimony, but because the disciples "saw" the Lord.

26   Hooker, *Mark*, 387; Martin, *Mark*, 452.

27   Moloney, *Mark*, 349.

28   Moloney, *Mark*, 348-354. There is something very Pauline in what Mark is attempting to do; Paul holds that God has saved us by his free gift of grace, available through the death and resurrection of Jesus.

29   Moloney, *Resurrection*, 15.

30   Boring, *Mark*, 449. Dunn, *Jesus Remembered*, 832-833, n. 26, similarly: it is part of Mark's genius that he leaves his story open at the end, open for the congregations who hear it being read to carry it on from what they know happened thereafter and what they know from personal experience is still happening. Pagola, *Jesus*, 416-17, suggests that as readers we are invited to return to the beginning of the story, and from the perspective of the resurrection, reflect on it anew, and come to 'see' the real identity of Jesus and the profound content of his activity and message. Martin, *Mark*, 453, states that it is left to the readers to live and proclaim the message entrusted to the women; McBride, *Mark*, 264-65.

31   Malbon, *Company*, 62-67.

32   Pope Francis, *Christus Vivit,* 37, suggests how young people can help to keep the Church young. "Young people can offer the Church the beauty of youth by renewing her ability to 'rejoice with new beginnings, to give unreservedly of herself, to be renewed and to set out for ever greater accomplishments.'"

PART II

A Prayer and Parables

So far in our book we have been considering episodes in which Jesus has personally encountered young people, and we have reflected on what we can learn from them about Jesus, about young people, and about our own discipleship. In this second part of the book I would like to examine four occasions in which Jesus refers to young people in his teaching: his prayer to the Father, and three parables: the parable of the two sons ("Yes" and "No"), the parable about youngsters playing in the market place (dance and dirge), and the parable of the two lost sons.

Chapter Eleven

The Prayer of Jesus

This prayer of thanksgiving is found both in Luke (10:21-22) and Matthew (11:25-27). I shall follow Luke's version in this chapter. Its context is the early part of the lengthy central section of Luke's story of Jesus, usually referred to as the journey to Jerusalem or the travel narrative. The evangelist uses this journey motif from 9:51-19:27 as a kind of framework within which he can explore salient aspects of discipleship, the way of Jesus.[1] Throughout this major block of material, mainly devoted to the teaching of Jesus, there are many clear reminders of the journey theme.[2]

As the journey gets under way, Jesus sends messengers ahead of him. They go to a Samaritan village to prepare for his coming, but the villagers are not interested in receiving him because he is going up to Jerusalem. This reflects the prejudice and animosity which existed between Samaritans and Jews at the time. James and John wish to respond in kind and ask Jesus whether they should call down fire from heaven to burn them up, a suggestion which incurs a rebuke from the Master. As they journey on, there are three brief encounters which highlight the radical demands of discipleship. After this, Jesus appoints seventy-two disciples and sends them on mission to the places he is to visit on his journey. He later speaks with some sadness and in tones of warning about the lakeside towns for their lack of response. The seventy-two then return from their mission. They are delighted with what they have been able to do in Jesus' name. He states that they should rejoice rather that their names are written in heaven.[3]

> At that same hour Jesus rejoiced in the Holy Spirit and said, 'I thank you, Father, Lord of heaven and earth, because you have hidden these things from the wise and the intelligent and have revealed them to infants; yes, Father, for such was your gracious will. All things have been handed over to me by my Father; and no one knows who the Son is except the Father, or who the Father is except the Son and anyone to whom the Son chooses to reveal him.'
>
> Then turning to the disciples, Jesus said to them privately, 'Blessed are the eyes that see what you see! For I tell you that many prophets and kings desired to see what you see, but did not see it, and to hear what you hear, but did not hear it.' (10:21–24)

The joy from the previous episode concerning mission, to which this section is closely tied, spills over, as Jesus immediately bursts into joyful prayer. He does so under the inspiration or influence of the Spirit, whose anointing had been such a significant aspect at his baptism, and in whose name he had launched his mission in the Nazareth synagogue.[4] Already Luke has several times referred to the prayer of Jesus: Jesus prays at the baptism, withdraws on occasion to quiet places, prays before the call of the Twelve, before Peter's profession of faith, and at the transfiguration.[5] Shortly after the episode we are considering, stimulated by the sight of him at prayer, the disciples will ask to be taught how to pray, and Jesus will give them their own special prayer, the "Our Father".[6]

This time Luke does not simply state that Jesus prays, but provides the reader with the content of his prayer. The language is poetic, has a strong Semitic ring, and follows the pattern of synagogue prayers of praise and thanksgiving; Jesus is adopting the language of the psalmists.[7] Jesus addresses God both as "Father", and "Lord of heaven and earth", a form of address which at the same time acknowledges God's transcendence and otherness, and also his closeness, care and intimacy.[8] "Father" occurs here five times, "Son" three. Jesus thanks God for choosing both to conceal and to reveal.[9] The message of the Kingdom's presence, made known by the words and works of Jesus, has been hidden from the wise and intelligent religious specialists,[10] but has been made known to ordinary people, the "little ones". The Greek word used here is *nēpios*, meaning infant. So "babies are singled out as recipients of divine revelation."[11] Jesus recognises that this is God's good pleasure, God's way, which subverts traditional Jewish religious thinking. God's predilection for the poor, the lowly and needy, those without influence, God's paradoxical tendency to overturn normal human values, expectations and priorities, is a theme which Luke highlights throughout his Gospel. Mary celebrates this reversal motif in the *Magnificat*, and from the outset of his ministry, Jesus has set out to bring the good news to the poor and outsiders.[12]

Jesus moves on to reveal the relationship which stands at the basis of his prayer. Speaking in language which has a distinctly Johannine ring,[13] he shares his awareness of his unique identity and his role, his intimate relationship with the Father as Son. The sovereign Father has gifted him with authority.[14] He is uniquely known in the depth of his being by the Father, and he knows the Father as no other does. The relationship is reciprocal. And so, he alone is able to reveal the Father, and does so to those whom he chooses.[15] That choice is an expression of love and is a free gift. Recalling Jesus' words at the age of twelve (2:49) and the divine reassurances in the baptism and transfiguration scenes, it would seem that "primary in Luke's presentation of Jesus is also a sense of a unique relationship with God into which he wishes to draw human beings."[16]

Jesus next addresses the chosen disciples privately, proclaiming them blessed and happy because of what they can hear and see.[17] For they, ordinary and lowly as they are, are privileged to be living in a special time, the time of revelation, the time longed for over centuries by the prophets and kings of old, the most religious and powerful people of Israel's history. They have seen God's works in Jesus' healing ministry and heard God's words in his preaching. They are witnessing now the fulfilment of Israel's dreams in the presence and ministry of Jesus; for God's Kingdom is manifest wherever Jesus is present.[18] They have been able to recognise and appreciate this also through their recent participation in his mission.

Reflections

As followers of Jesus we are joyful people, and our joy stems from the realisation that we have been so remarkably blessed. For we know that what the prophets of old longed for and dreamed about, longings and dreams articulated in so many beautiful Old Testament extracts used often in our liturgical readings, have been fulfilled in Jesus. In a very true and profound sense, our eyes have seen, and our ears have heard. We have come to share something of the experience of Jesus' early disciples, as they listened to his words and witnessed what he was doing. For all our ordinariness and weakness and mistakes, we are aware of the revelation of God's saving love, God's compassion and faithfulness. That awareness has come to us through God's gracious good pleasure. We come under the description used by Jesus in his prayer: "infants".

As Christians we are all called to be people of prayer. We turn to God in praise and thanksgiving because we have been embraced by the Kingdom; we live and move and have our being in the heart of God. We need to allow this to sink in and permeate the whole of our being. Its implications are immense. It means that every aspect of our lives is drawn into the circle of God's love. There is nothing 'ordinary' anymore. All our activities, be they humdrum and mundane, or exciting and creative, have a new dimension—washing up, cleaning the house, gardening, playing games, preparing lectures or classes, sitting at traffic lights, cooking a meal, practising the guitar—everything now has enormous significance, for it is caught up in our relationship with God.

In his prayer as recorded here by Luke, Jesus addresses God as *Abba, Father*. Drawn into this intimate relationship, we, too, can adopt this way of speaking to God, as his beloved daughters and sons. There is a wonderful familiarity about our prayer. In his prayer Jesus also acknowledges the otherness of God, who is Lord of heaven and earth, the God "beyond all names".[19] And it is important for us to maintain this dimension too. Like Moses at the burning bush, realising that we tread on holy ground, we take off our sandals.[20] There is respect and deep reverence in the presence of the utterly Other. Familiarity and reverence are the two wings of our relationship with our God, two ongoing aspects of our prayer.

A friend of mine has often in conversation spoken of the natural ability of infants to pray, to cope easily and comfortably with a little silence, and actually enjoy it. It is tragic that, as they grow, they forget, lose, or fail to develop the facility to pray. The sense of God's presence and love can fade, and even disappear. Perhaps we, as educators, have failed them here. In schools, when it is a question of worship and prayer, the default option can be Mass. But if our young people no longer have a real relationship with God in prayer, they will inevitably find Mass quite meaningless. More attention needs to be paid to fostering that relationship with God, perhaps also by creating other forms of worship.[21]

Maybe part of the problem is our lack of confidence in our ability to help young people in this area. Perhaps the level of our awareness of being sons and daughters of God, our awareness of God's presence within us, is not buoyant enough to move us to share that relationship with our young people. We cannot reveal to them what we don't have or know personally. Our relationship with God is not an idea, it is an experience, an experience which is God's gift, an experience to be nourished and deepened by spending time in silent prayer. If we are genuinely men and women of prayer, comfortable with silence and stillness, young people will soon come to realise that. And if we are also deeply human and loving people, they will be drawn to what they see in us. And we, too, can reveal the Father and Jesus to the "little ones". But it is also true that if we are open and sensitive, the "little ones" can reveal something of God's mystery and God's ways to us. And there is something wonderful about this.

I chose this Gospel reading for my mother's funeral over thirty years ago. She had left school at the age of fifteen; in those days a tertiary education was unthinkable for working class folk. She taught me how to pray and gave me a sense of God's presence in my life. That's a wonderful gift. I always felt that she was much closer to God, more in tune with God's ways, than her priest, 'theologian' son.

Endnotes

1   "Now it happened that as the time drew near for him to be taken up, he resolutely turned his face towards Jerusalem..." (9:51) Some scholars maintain that the motif continues as far as 19:44.

2   At 9:57, "As they travelled along"; 10:38, "In the course of their journey he came to a village"; 13:22, "Through towns and villages he went"; 17:11, "Now on the way to Jerusalem he travelled along the border between Samaria and Galilee"; 18:31, "Now we are going up to Jerusalem"; 19:11, "He was near Jerusalem"; 19:28, "He went on ahead, going up to Jerusalem"; 19:37, "And now, as he was approaching the downward slope of the Mount of Olives"; 19:41, "As he drew near and came in sight of the city"; 19:45, "Then he went into the Temple."

3   In Matthew, the context of Jesus' prayer to the Father is failure, for it follows his reproaching the cities in which he had worked for their unwillingness to be converted. Bartholomé, *Los Niños,* 193, suggests that our apostolic failures, too, can lead us into deeper prayer and a richer understanding of God's ways.

4   Carroll, *Luke,* 240, notes that, though the Spirit has not been mentioned since then, Jesus engages in mission under the Spirit's empowerment.

5   3:21–22; 5:15; 6:12; 9:18; 9:28–29.

6   11:2-4. Other references to the prayer of Jesus occur in the Passion Narrative: Jesus prays for Simon Peter at the Supper (22:31-34); the agony prayer on the Mount of Olives (22:39-46); the Calvary prayer of forgiveness (23:34); Jesus' dying prayer (23:46). Luke provides us with a number of sayings and parables of Jesus concerning prayer: the parable of the friend at midnight (11:5-8); sayings about asking and seeking (11:9-13); the parable of the judge and the widow (18:1-8); the parable of the Pharisee and the tax collector (18:9-14); the exhortation to his disciples to pray and not lose heart (18:1); the exhortation in Jerusalem (21:36); the exhortation on the Mount of Olives (22:40).

7   Robert C. Tannehill, *Luke,* (Nashville: Abingdon Press, 1996), 179. Many psalms contain the words "I thank you that... " followed by the reason (Ps 78:1;

138:1); this is the pattern also of the *Magnificat* and *Benedictus* earlier in the Gospel; see Johnson, *Luke,* 169; Green, *Luke,* 422. Marshall, *Luke,* 432, detects in this section a background of Jewish wisdom literature.

8   Marshall, *Luke,* 433, holds that Jesus uses the *Abba* address to the Father, as do children to their dad.

9   Marshall, *Luke,* 434, suggests that the concealing is perhaps not to be stressed: "What was happening remained obscure in its significance to one group of people, but to the disciples it constituted a revelation of God's saving action."

10   The religious elite of Jesus' day, despite their learning, have failed to recognise what is happening in Jesus. Carroll, *Luke,* 240, observes that they are wise and knowledgeable but not discerning about the ways of God.

11   Carroll, *Luke,* 241. Tannehill, *Luke,* 179, refers to those who are infants in knowledge. McBride, *Luke,* 137, puts it this way: "Jesus goes to the nursery of the world to choose his followers."

12   1:51–53; 4:18–19; see also 1 Cor 1:18–31: "not many of you were wise by human standards, not many were powerful, not many were of noble birth…"

13   See especially John chapter 17, the prayer of Jesus at the Supper.

14   The verb "handed over" can be used of the handing down of knowledge or the transfer of power and authority. Marshall, *Luke,* 436, believes that probably both authority and knowledge are meant here.

15   Some scholars, G.H.P. Thompson, *The Gospel According to Luke* (Oxford: Clarendon Press, 1972), 163, amongst them, think that the relationship between God and Israel (described as father and son) is in the background.

16   Byrne, *Hospitality,* 97. Tannehill, *Luke,* 180, notes that in the cultural context "father" may carry connotations of authority; it also connotes an intimacy and love that can be trusted.

17   In Matthew the next verses are presented in a different context, after the parable of the sower (13:16–17). This is the seventh *macarism* or beatitude of the Gospel. Instead, he includes the invitation of Jesus: "Come to me all you who are weary, and are carrying heavy burdens, and I will give you rest. Take my yoke upon you, and learn from me; for I am gentle and humble in heart, and you will find rest for your souls. For my yoke is easy and my burden is light" (11:28–30).

18   Green, *Luke,* 423–424.

19   As in the hymn *God, Beyond All Names* by Bernadette Farrell.

20   Exod 3:5.

21   Pope Francis, *Christus Vivit,* 224, states that "we should never underestimate the ability of young people to be open to contemplative prayer. We need only find the right ways and means to help them embark on this precious experience."

Chapter Twelve

Dance and Dirge

There is an interesting parable of Jesus, found in both Matthew and Luke, in which he draws important lessons from the behaviour of children. I shall follow Luke's version, though the differences between the two are very minor. In the Lukan context, Jesus recounts this story early in his ministry after he has healed the centurion's servant and raised to life the son of the widow of Nain. It seems that the disciples of John the Baptist have become aware of the activities of Jesus and his teaching, and so have gleaned a great deal of information to communicate to their Master, now in prison (3:19–20), concerning what Jesus has been saying and doing, and the way in which people are responding to him.[1] It is clear that there is a discrepancy between the style and outlook of the Baptist and that of Jesus.

> So John summoned two of his disciples and sent them to the Lord to ask, 'Are you the one who is to come, or are we to wait for another?' When the men had come to him, they said, 'John the Baptist has sent us to you to ask, "Are you the one who is to come, or are we to wait for another?"' Jesus had just then[2] cured many people of diseases, plagues, and evil spirits, and had given sight to many who were blind. And he answered them, 'Go and tell John what you have seen and heard: the blind receive their sight, the lame walk, the lepers are cleansed, the deaf hear, the dead are raised, the poor have good news brought to them. And blessed is anyone who takes no offence at me.' (Luke 7: 19–23)

Earlier in the story the reader is informed about the preaching of the Baptist near the Jordan, in which he refers to "the wrath to come", and "the axe lying at the root of the trees" (3:7–9). As the precursor, he describes the one coming after him as baptising, not with water like him, but with the Holy Spirit and fire. "His winnowing fork is in his hand, to clear the threshing floor and to gather the wheat into his granary; but the chaff he will burn with unquenchable fire."[3] John is expecting imminent eschatological judgement, the overthrowing of wrong and evil. The tone and emphasis in the words of Jesus are different, as is evident in his inaugural sermon in Nazareth.[4] The activities he is engaged in, healing and exorcising, are also different, as are the people with whom he mixes. This puzzles the Baptist and spurs him to seek clarification as to whether Jesus is the figure he envisaged. So, he sends two of his disciples[5] to put the crucial question concerning Jesus' identity in blunt terms: "Are you the one who is to come, or are we to wait for another?" Two was the normally accepted number for genuine witnesses.

The disciples do what they have been asked to do, repeating John's question verbatim. In the meantime, Jesus has been continuing his healing activity, and so in answer, rather than a simple "yes" or "no", he points his visitors to what has been happening, and what they themselves have witnessed: blind people see, the lame can now walk, lepers are cleansed, folk who were deaf can hear again, the dead are raised to life. These phrases strongly echo the messianic expectations of the prophet Isaiah.[6] The evidence is clear, and points to the presence of the promised eschatological salvation. And he adds in the place of emphasis that the poor and ordinary people have been brought good news. His final comment, while couched in general terms, is something of a challenge to his interlocutors: "Blessed is anyone who has taken no offence at me." Jesus is aware that John is struggling to come to terms with the unexpected style of his ministry; he is sensitive to his perplexity.[7] The messengers are left to draw their own conclusions and report back.[8]

The response of Jesus throws the burden of accurate discernment back to the Baptist. One issue is to clarify the kind of "coming one" he was expecting or hoping for. If the message and activities of Jesus measure up, the Baptist has his answer: he need not wait for another. If there is a discrepancy, Jesus indirectly invites him to think again before dismissing him, and not be put off by his quite different approach and style. The prophecies really are being fulfilled.

The Baptist's disciples leave. We are not informed of John's response. In their absence the narrative moves on, as Jesus speaks positively to the crowds about John:

> 'What did you go out into the wilderness to look at? A reed shaken by the wind? What then did you go out to see? Someone dressed in soft robes? Look, those who put on fine clothing and live in luxury are in royal palaces.

What then did you go out to see? A prophet? Yes, I tell you, and more than a prophet. This is the one about whom it is written, "See, I am sending my messenger ahead of you, who will prepare your way before you." I tell you, among those born of women no one is greater than John; yet the least in the kingdom of God is greater than he.' (And all the people who heard this, including the tax-collectors, acknowledged the justice of God, because they had been baptized with John's baptism. But by refusing to be baptized by him, the Pharisees and the lawyers rejected God's purpose for themselves.) (Luke 7:24–30)

"In spite of the deep gulf that separated his radiant friendliness from John's forbidding austerity, Jesus had a profound appreciation of his grim herald."[9] Jesus recalls the way in which the crowds went out into the wilderness by the Jordan river to encounter John.[10] The reeds by the riverside, being blown about by the wind, have little to offer, nor are they an accurate reflection of the Baptist, who was anything but wavering or uncertain. Nor was he the kind of person dressed in fine clothing and living in luxury, who might create something of a stir. He was known to be an ascetic. What they were interested in was to meet a prophet, a man of strength and conviction,[11] a person who proclaims the word of God clearly. In this their estimation was correct. But Jesus goes on to assert even more. Quoting Malachi he presents the Baptist as the one sent by God to prepare the way for the "coming one."[12]

The final statement of Jesus is challenging. No one who has ever been born is greater than he—amazing praise indeed.[13] However, "that to which John's ministry pointed and for which it prepared has broken into the world, so that conventional ways of measuring honour and status have been inverted."[14] The least of those who are already entering the dawning Kingdom have greater standing than he. The distinction between old and new reality, promise and fulfilment, is telling. The Baptist, for all his importance, belongs to the past era, he is a transitional figure.[15] The evangelist concludes with a parenthesis, observing that many of Jesus' listeners, some of whom were even tax-collectors, had recognised John as a prophet from God and received John's baptism, and on hearing Jesus, praised God. Such people are open to Jesus too. The religious elite, on the other hand, who rejected him, are rejecting God's saving purpose—a strong statement.[16] What was true for John is true for Jesus. "The work of God is there to be seen and heard, but not all will discern."[17]

Jesus continues to address the crowds using a parable which refers to young people:

'To what then will I compare the people of this generation, and what are they like? They are like children sitting in the marketplace and calling to one another, "We played the flute for you, and you did not dance; we wailed, and you did not weep." For John the Baptist has come eating no bread and drinking no wine, and you say, "He has a demon"; the Son of Man has come eating and drinking, and you say, "Look, a glutton and a drunkard, a friend of tax-collectors and sinners!" Nevertheless, wisdom is vindicated by all her children.' (Luke 7:31–35)

Having just pondered the identity and role of both the Baptist and Jesus, this section highlights the response of the people to both figures sent by God, whilst incidentally giving us more information about Jesus' style of ministry and his priorities. Jesus refers to "this generation", which is almost a technical term to describe his contemporaries. The pejorative term is rooted in the Old Testament, where it is applied to the people who were led by Moses through the wilderness, attached to such descriptors as "faithless, evil, sinful, perverse, crooked."[18] The people of Jesus' time are seen to have much in common with the people of the time of Noah and of Moses.

Jesus is an acute observer of what takes place around him. In the parable he uses on this occasion, he likens the people's responses to the Baptist and himself to what happens in the social centre of the marketplace where children are sitting around, yelling to one another and playing games. The structure of the brief parable is carefully orchestrated in parallels, a characteristic feature of Hebrew poetry: the piping and the refusal to dance; the wailing and the refusal to mourn. Similarly, the twofold application of the parable has a parallel structure: John does not eat or drink, inviting a critical response; Jesus does eat and drink, inviting a critical response.[19]

The precise nature of the game is unclear. It could be that one group of children is active and wants to play at weddings, but the other group refuses to join in. So, the same active group then changes key and wishes to play at funerals, and again the others are unwilling to participate. Alternatively, one group is keen on playing at weddings, the other at funerals, and neither will budge.[20] Yet another interpretation stresses the word "sitting".[21] One group of children is sitting around and tries to get the others first to dance and then to mourn. The other group is non-cooperative, and the first cohort ridicules them as spoilsports.

There are different ways of interpreting the parable too.[22] Some view the youngsters who are seated as representing "this generation". They give orders, announce the games, attempt to dictate the play, and call the tune, demanding that John and then Jesus should fall in with their agendas, script and whims. In different ways both John and Jesus have been unwilling to accede to their demands, to modify or adapt their message and style of ministry; they have remained true to their vision of their mission.[23] Alternatively, others see the active children as representing Jesus and the Baptist respectively. Jesus calls for celebration and John for repentance. The people, "this generation", ignore them both.[24]

In his presentation, Jesus highlights the differences between the Baptist and himself. John was an ascetic, with a harsh and demanding lifestyle, an unusual appearance, and a message of repentance laced with threats of imminent fiery judgement. The people were critical and labelled him as crazy or, equivalently in that culture, as possessed by a devil, a comment which was levelled also at Jesus on occasion.[25] The people at the time preferred dancing and celebration. Jesus himself, on the other hand, comes along with a very different message and style.[26] He emphasises God's compassion, acceptance and forgiveness. He enjoys a meal, is partial to a drink, and mixes freely in friendship with dishonest tax-gatherers and sinners. This causes raised eyebrows, strong criticism, deep scandal and rejection; dancing and celebration are jettisoned for puritanical mourning. It seems, then, that whatever kind of prophet God sends to his people, offering them a way to salvation, they are unwilling to respond positively; they are not prepared to welcome and to participate in what is being freely offered.[27]

The final comment attributed to Jesus is rather obscure: "And yet wisdom is vindicated by all her children."[28] In the original statement "Wisdom" probably refers to God and God's plan of salvation, revealed by John and Jesus. Despite the rejection by Israel of God's final prophets, John and Jesus, God's saving plan will finally win through. John and Jesus are Wisdom's children, and those who respond positively to their teaching, especially that of Jesus, will also become Wisdom's children.[29] The words of Jesus are a shout of victory. The responsibility for failure to recognise Jesus' identity and accept his message rests squarely with his contemporaries. "The compelling evidence of what Jesus has done is not impaired by the perversity of its reception."[30]

Reflections

In this parable an ordinary situation of children at play is used by Jesus in order to highlight a fundamental problem in salvation history: the fact that, despite their different message and style, both he and the Baptist before him have met misunderstanding, criticism and rejection, especially on the part of the religious leadership. The tragedy was that it was God's saving approach in love that was being rejected, God's offer of new life and transformation.

People had their own agendas and were closed to the wonderful gift on offer. They allowed their preconceived ideas, their expectations and prejudices to make them deaf to the message of salvation, blind to the expressions of God's saving presence in Jesus. They risked missing out on the most important and wonderful thing they could possibly experience.

Things don't change with the passing of the years and in cultures of a different kind! In our mission today, as disciples of Jesus and members of the Christian community, the Church, we are often faced with a similar negative response. Often the people of our generation, even the young ones, fail to respond with enthusiasm to our message, our values and way of living.[31] The increasing emptiness of our churches can be disconcerting. Even when we seek to be creative in our evangelising, results are rarely encouraging. We may be forgiven for feeling as Jesus did. Yet Jesus did not give up. He trusted in the Father's merciful love. And so, we must continue to reach out in compassion and kindness to all, continue to bear witness to the way of Jesus, not be preoccupied with success and results, do our best and leave it all in God's gracious hands. God's love will always be there for us and for everyone.

I'm sure that we have all witnessed situations in which young people find it hard to agree, situations when some can be petulant, stubborn, awkward, uncooperative and so on. Mood swings are not uncommon. This can be difficult to deal with. More widely, the young people of the parable capture and highlight so vividly our broader human experience of finding ourselves in no-win situations. In marriage with our partner, in dealings with our children or ageing parents, in our workplaces, with our friends, in ministry and leadership, in games and sport, there are times when whatever we do is wrong. It can be so frustrating and so disheartening. At least we can be aware that Jesus knows how we feel! Perhaps we need to make sure that we don't lose our sense of humour. Life can be like this! But it isn't always one-way traffic. We all have the capacity to be spoilsports and wreckers, to withdraw our cooperation and to sulk. When we catch ourselves playing this role, perhaps it's good to ask ourselves why, what is it all about at a deeper level. If we are open and honest with ourselves, we can learn a lot about ourselves. And then we can do something to rectify our attitudes and behaviour and be people who are positive, constructive and creatively optimistic. And this will help us to understand others better and to reach out to help in more appropriate ways.

Another tendency which a certain understanding of the parable reveals is the desire to control, to dictate what's going on, to call the tune, to impose on others, to get our own way, and then to complain bitterly when we don't succeed in our self-centred endeavours. Sometimes such tendencies can be executed with great subtlety and skill, sometimes with a certain bluff clumsiness. In any case, such behaviour betrays a lack of respect for the value and individuality and freedom of others. This can be true of young people as they grow to maturity, but it is more serious when those responsible are adults. Often people are not aware when they manifest these tendencies. Helping them demands skill and sensitivity.

Finally, the parable invites us to ponder our own response to Jesus and his way. There can be the danger of a certain selectivity in the way we respond to the demands of discipleship. Perhaps at times we feel drawn to the Baptist's blunt, black-and-white approach rather than the more nuanced, patient and gentle style of Jesus. In our Church today there are certainly those who are critical of Pope Francis' informal, deeply human, compassionate interpretation of the way of Jesus, preferring instead a more rigorous, legalistic, exclusivist, formal, even clerical way of Christian living. Amongst them one sometimes comes across young people, too, attracted to formalism and security. Perhaps we can ask ourselves where we stand, and why. And we need to pray for openness and wisdom.

Endnotes

1   John's being in prison is not mentioned here as it is in the Matthaean parallel (11:16–19); Luke has mentioned it earlier in 3:20. Green, *Luke,* 294, notes the close link with what has just been narrated (7:1–17).

2   Green, *Luke,* 296, prefers "in that hour" to the NRSV "just then", for Luke uses this phrase at important moments of the narrative; also, Johnson, *Luke,* 122.

3   3:7–17; in 3:16 the Baptist speaks of the "one more powerful than I" (the Messiah) who is coming.

4   4:6–21. Green, *Luke,* 295, notes that "John's interest lies on the fault line between his eschatological expectations and the realities of Jesus' performance."

5   The presence of disciples who are aloof from the movement of Jesus is an indication that the Baptist is not convinced of Jesus' role: (Caird, *Luke,* 111; McBride, *Luke,* 99). Tannehill, *Luke,* 130, points out that two are required for reliable witness (Deut 19:15).

6   Isa 61:1; 35:5–6; 26:19; 29:18–19; 42:18; 43:8. Green, *Luke,* 297, refers to this as "a symphony of Isaian echoes", and observes that the "overlap with Jesus' inaugural sermon and his answer to John provides a powerful sanction for the integrity of his mission: he is doing what the Spirit of the Lord anointed him to do."

Marshall, *Luke*, 291, notes that the list refers to the ministry of Jesus as a whole, and is couched in the language of the Old Testament.

7   Byrne, *Hospitality*, 71; Caird, *Luke*, 112. McBride, *Luke*, 98, calls this "a delicate plea for understanding".

8   Marshall, *Luke*, 287, observes that "the person who recognises the fulfilment will know that Jesus is the coming One, and will not be put off by his failure to live up to the traditional—or Johannine—expectations."

9   Caird, *Luke*, 111.

10   The Greek could also be rendered: *Why did you go...?* See Evans, *Luke*, 353.

11   Marshall, *Luke*, 292.

12   Mal 3:1 and also Exod 23:20; John is the end-time prophet proclaimed in scripture. The "you" now refers to Jesus. The quotation is also found in Mark 1:2; Matthew 11:10.

13   Carroll, *Luke*, 172, refers to Jesus' unequivocal affirmation of John as a prophet. Caird, *Luke*, 111, points out that Jesus' public testimony to the prophetic greatness of the Baptist entailed the risk of reprisals from Herod.

14   Green, *Luke*, 299; Carroll, *Luke*, 172.

15   Byrne, *Hospitality*, 72; Carroll, *Luke*, 172. Caird, *Luke*, 112: "John belonged to the old order—the greatest man who ever lived before the coming of the kingdom."

16   McBride, *Luke*, 99; Marshall, *Luke*, 297; Eugene LaVerdiere, *Luke* (Dublin: Veritas, 1980), 106, take these verses as an introduction to what follows. Johnson, *Luke*, 125, holds that the words are Luke's "authorial commentary" rather than a report of Jesus' words. He also notes that the "division in the people" evinced here was predicted by Simeon.

17   Carroll, *Luke*, 171.

18   Deut 1:35; 32:5, 20; Ps 78:8. Jesus adopts this phrase in a number of situations: Luke 9:41; 11:29–32; 11:50–51; 17:25. See Meier, 2:145.

19   The overall structure takes a crossover or chiastic format: joy, sorrow, sorrow, joy. See Meier, *A Marginal Jew*, 2:147–148; Byrne, *Hospitality*, 72. Both parable and application are structured according to antithetical parallelism.

20   Meier, *A Marginal Jew*, 2:147.

21   Jeremias, *The Parables of Jesus* (London, SCM 1972), 160–162. Barbara E. Reid, *Parables for Preachers (Year C)* (Collegeville, MN: Liturgical Press, 2000), 274, n. 11, suggests that this is the way in which Matthew sees it, and "it is likely that Luke also is to be understood this way."

22   See Davies & Allison, *Matthew*, 180; Meier, *Matthew*, 123; H. B. Green, *Matthew*, 117.

23   Jeremias, *Parables*, 160–162; Meier, *A Marginal Jew*, 2:148; Carroll, *Luke*, 173; Green, *Luke*, 303: John and Jesus "are rejected for not following the conventions determined and propagated by religious people who claim that those conventions are divinely sanctioned."

24 Meier, *A Marginal Jew*, 148. Reid, *Parables*, 274, writes: "This generation responded neither to John's "dirge" nor Jesus' "flute"." She suggests the imagery of court proceedings: the marketplace (Acts 16:19), "sitting", to "call out" (Luke 23:20; Acts 21:40; 22:2). The invitation is not a game; there are serious consequences for those refusing the invitation made by John and Jesus.

25 Mark 3:21.

26 Meier, *A Marginal Jew*, 2:152, suggests that Jesus is consciously using the "Son of Man", probably the most problematic title for Jesus in the whole Gospel tradition, as a riddle-like, parable-like, mind-teasing self-designation.

27 Meier, *A Marginal Jew*, 2:149: "The result is spiritual paralysis and an apparent frustration of God's saving plan to rescue his chosen people in this last hour of their history."

28 Matthew 11:19 has "by her deeds". Scholars maintain that Luke is probably nearer the original. On this see Meier, *A Marginal Jew*, 2:153. He writes "The affirmation that wisdom is or will be vindicated, coming as it does right after two glaring examples of how God's prophets are rejected by God's people, suggests that the introductory *kai* ("and") has an adversative sense and should be translated "and yet".

29 Byrne, *Hospitality*, 73; Green, *Luke*, 304. Evans, *Luke*, 359, does not accept that this may refer to John and Jesus; similarly, Marshall, *Luke* 304. Meier, *A Marginal Jew*, 2:153, believes that though John and Jesus are yoked together as two prophets of wisdom, the focus of the saying is on the "all" who heed them.

30 H. B. Green, *Matthew*, 118.

31 In *Christus Vivit*, 39–40, Pope Francis acknowledges that to many young people, God, religion and the Church seem empty words. Many do not see the Church as significant in their lives; they find the presence of the Church a nuisance, an irritant. Amongst the possible reasons for this, he lists sexual and financial scandals; a clergy ill-prepared to engage effectively with the sensitivities of the young; lack of care in homily preparation and the presentation of the word of God; the passive role assigned to the young within the Christian community; the Church's difficulty in explaining her doctrine and ethical positions to contemporary society.

Chapter Thirteen

Yes and No

After Matthew's Jesus has entered Jerusalem in triumph on what we call Palm Sunday, he clears the temple of those buying and selling there and overturns the tables of the money changers. Next day he returns to the temple after his initial bruising encounter with the religious leaders. Controversy continues, as Matthew follows Mark in presenting episodes in which the religious leaders challenge Jesus with questions about his authority, paying taxes to the emperor, the resurrection, the first commandment. Jesus raises with them the topic of the identity of David's son. Within this block of material Matthew includes a trilogy of parables: the parable of the two sons, the parable of the wicked tenants and the parable of the wedding banquet.[1] In the first of these, found only in Matthew,[2] the figure of the Baptist is again mentioned, as a link is forged with the preceding story in which his name and baptising role occur. The text reads:

> 'What do you think? A man had two sons; he went to the first and said, "Son, go and work in the vineyard today." He answered, "I will not"; but later he changed his mind and went. The father went to the second and said the same; and he answered, "I go, sir"; but he did not go. Which of the two did the will of his father?' They said, 'The first.' Jesus said to them, 'Truly I tell you, the tax-collectors and the prostitutes are going into the kingdom of God ahead of you. For John came to you in the way of righteousness and you did not believe him, but the tax-collectors and the prostitutes believed him; and even after you saw it, you did not change your minds and believe him.' (Matt 21:28–32)

Jesus, an accomplished teacher, engages his audience with a question, which is rhetorical: "What do you think?" He then presents a homely scenario. A father with two sons asks each in turn to go and do some work in tending the vineyard.³ He addresses the first son (*teknon*), probably the elder, with his request.⁴ Surprisingly, he responds with a blunt refusal: "I will not." Such disobedience is culturally unacceptable. But later he has a change of mind and heart, and goes along to carry out his father's request.⁵ By contrast, the other son shows great respect to his father, addressing him as "Lord", and immediately promises to do his bidding: "Of course." But he has no intention of complying; there is no mention of his changing his mind; his words are empty.⁶ Jesus puts a second question to his audience: "Which of the two did the will of his father?" And they are obliged to provide the correct, but incriminating answer: "The first."

In itself, the parable could have originally been a defence of Jesus' ministry to the outcasts and sinners in the face of criticism from the religious elite. It could also illustrate the split between saying and doing, which often occurs in our lives.⁷ However, with the application which Jesus here provides, the parable continues his polemic against the religious authorities. Jesus shocks them by identifying them as actors in the parable drama. Mention of a vineyard may symbolically represent Israel or the Kingdom.⁸ The tax-collectors and prostitutes, the disqualified, who are despised and banished to the religious periphery, are in fact now entering God's Kingdom first. Initially, their lifestyle suggested a refusal to obey God's will as expressed in the Law. When the Baptist came, however, these were the ones who repented and responded positively to his message. The religious leaders, highly respected and powerful men, expert in the requirements of the Law, initially refused to believe in John, the prophet sent by God, refused to accept his invitation to conversion and, unlike the first son, did not change their mind even when they saw the radical change in the lives of those viewed as 'sinners'. "The way of righteousness" has to do with responding generously to God's approach and demands, by a change of mind, heart and lifestyle, and so fulfilling God's will.⁹

What was true of the Baptist is true of Jesus. Those on the margins of organised religion, considered 'sinners' by the religious elite, have been the ones who have responded to Jesus' approach, his message, his openness and compassion. They have welcomed the in-break of the Kingdom. Those who felt comfortable and secure in their traditional religiosity, however, especially the leaders, have been unwilling to move out of their normal parameters into the new reality which Jesus is introducing.¹⁰ Entering the Kingdom "before you" may really mean "instead of you".¹¹ The leaders of Israel in Jesus' day continue the tradition of rejecting the prophets sent to them by God.

Reflections

In this parable Jesus uses older young people as a way of illustrating the important issue of response to God's approach through his presence and ministry. The two are clearly contrasted. Often that is true of siblings, be they male and/or female. Jesus is very much aware of what can happen in family relationships. It is not difficult for us to identify with the three characters in the story. As parents, pastors, educators, we have all been in the position of asking others to do something for us. Sometimes the response has been a refusal, and this is hard to take. We feel disappointed, hurt, let down, rejected, angry—a whole gamut of emotions. A transformation, like a mini resurrection, occurs when the individual changes his/her mind and fulfils our request. Sometimes, on the other hand, the response to our request has seemed like an enthusiastic or generous "yes", that wonderful little word of acceptance, empathy, cooperation. This makes us feel good, and maybe relieves some anxiety or hesitation. And then there follows the shock of realising that the "yes" has come to nothing, and we experience another range of uncomfortable emotions. Adults, as well as children, are capable of both types of response, as we know. How we handle these situations always presents a challenge. Do we shrug and let the situation pass, or react with a reprimand or with a gentle question? It is always good to express our thanks and appreciation or to offer reasons for our requests.

Looking back on our lives we may recall occasions when we have been the ones to refuse to do what has been asked of us: "No way!" We have probably felt that the request was unfair or unreasonable, too demanding, or inconvenient. But later, we've thought better of it, and decided to abandon our negativity and our upset feelings and carry out the request made of us. Sometimes the acceptance has been rather grudging, sometimes more generous. Or perhaps we are aware of occasions when we have said "OK" for peace in the house, for a quiet life, to humour someone, and our response has not been genuine and sincere. We have gone away and neglected to keep our word.

This parable, then, gives us an opportunity to think about the way we respond to requests made of us, the way in which we treat those who ask. It also challenges us to extrapolate a little and consider our response to God. This was the issue for Jesus in telling this parable. Perhaps in the past we have at times uttered an outright "no" to God's approach and God's demands, but then repented, changed mind and heart, and responded with love. Perhaps we need to make time and space to listen carefully for what God is asking of us today—through the words of scripture, through other people, through situations which crop up, through the world around us, through the longings deep in our hearts.

The parable also invites us to ponder whether we are prone to simply go through the motions of discipleship. We say a kind of "yes" to God but somehow don't quite get around to doing what is required. We procrastinate, we manufacture flimsy excuses, we develop avoidance techniques, effectively turning our "yes" into a "no". We are missing or wasting opportunities for growth, for generosity, for unselfishness. We are keeping God at a 'safe' distance, and in that case, we are only half alive, if that.

In Matthew's Gospel, Jesus several times stresses the importance of action rather than words. It is not the one who repeatedly invokes the Lord who will enter the Kingdom of heaven, "but the one who does the will of my Father in heaven" (7:21). The wise man who builds his house on a rock is one "who hears these words of mine and acts on them" (7:24). Those who do the heavenly Father's will become the brothers, sisters and mother of Jesus (12:50). In the parable of the Judgement, the emphasis in Jesus' words is on action that expresses care and concern for those in need (25:31-46). Perhaps our current parable also shows that God looks to the final outcome of our lives. "God can put up with an initial "No", and a lot of other "No's" (*sic*) besides, on the way to a final and lasting "Yes."[12] And there is always the danger that the righteous establishment, who appear to be religious and observant, should fail to understand the immense compassionate love and mercy of God, whereas those aware of their weakness and need can be open to God's free gift of the Kingdom.

Endnotes

1   The parable of the wicked tenants (21:33-46) is found in Mark (12:1-12) and Luke (20:9-19); Luke has a rather different version of the banquet parable in 14:16-24.

2   There are three different manuscript versions of the parable. For details see Green, *Matthew*, 178; Harrington, *Matthew*, 299; Senior, *Matthew*, 237; Meier, *Matthew*, 240; Beare, *Matthew* 424. Most scholars concur with the NRSV.

3   Senior, *Matthew*, 237, notes that mention of the vineyard links this parable with the one which follows.

4   Davies & Allison, *Matthew*, 359, hold that *teknon* here means "child", a form of familiar address, a term of affection, which makes the subsequent refusal more dramatic. Luz, *Matthew*, 3:25, also uses "child" in his translation.

5   The verb *metamelomai* means to change one's mind; Luz, 3:30, suggests that here it probably implies that he was sorry. Hagner, *Matthew*, 2:613, says "regret".

6   Davies & Allison, *Matthew*, 360. They note that Jesus' opponents are adept at laying traps but not at avoiding falling into them themselves. Jesus is much cleverer on both scores.

7   Meier, *Matthew*, 240; see 7:21–23; 12:50; 23:3–4.

8   Isa 5:1–7. Hagner, *Matthew*, 2:613; Senior, *Matthew*, 237; Meier, *Matthew*, 241, who suggests also the Kingdom. Davies & Allison, *Matthew*, 359, note the allegorical interpretation: the father represents God, the first son the 'sinners', the second son the chief priests and elders.

9   Luz, *Matthew*, 3:28, states: "The contrast between the two sons is designed to show that the issue is doing the will of God."

10   Meier, *Matthew*, 241, following Chrysostom, suggests a further meaning: those saying "yes" could be the Jews; those saying "no" but changing, the Gentiles. Davies & Allison, *Matthew*, 361, claim that modern exegetes prefer to think of believing and unbelieving Israel.

11   Meier, *Matthew*, 241; the two following parables have this thrust.

12   Byrne, *Lifting the Burden*, 161.

Chapter Fourteen

Two Lost Sons

My final parable is perhaps the most famous and most loved of all the parables of Jesus. It is found only in Luke's Gospel. The wider context for this is what is often referred to as the travel or journey narrative, as Jesus makes his way to Jerusalem. Luke uses the idea of a journey as a framework within which to explore aspects of Jesus' message concerning discipleship (9:51–19:27). The immediate context is an occasion when Jesus is sharing his table with people who are on the margins of religious society. For this he is criticised, not for the first time, by the religious elite.

The Setting (15:1–2)

> Now all the tax collectors and sinners were coming near to listen to him. And the Pharisees and the scribes were grumbling and saying, "This fellow welcomes sinners and eats with them." (15:1–2)

Though brief, this is a significant passage.[1] The religious outcasts and other outsiders who bear the social stigma of "sinners", "persons living outside the structure of faithful Torah observance",[2] are drawing close to Jesus. Jesus seems to be comfortable with people who would normally be excluded. They obviously feel comfortable with him. Their purpose is to listen to him, which suggests a level of openness to his person and his message.[3] In the background are the "Pharisees and scribes", who keep their distance to avoid contamination, and shun table fellowship with sinners.[4] They "grumble" repeatedly and openly.[5]

Their criticism is focused not only on Jesus' eating and drinking with these people, as on earlier occasions,[6] but also on his welcoming them, his offering them hospitality. To host or entertain sinners was a more serious offence in their eyes than simply to eat with sinners informally or to accept invitations, which was itself scandalous enough. In their eyes Jesus was welcoming the dregs of society.[7]

The table fellowship of Jesus, as it is called, his sharing meals with others, seems to have been a key feature of his ministry. In the villages of Galilee, where hospitality was an essential aspect of life, it was quite natural that Jesus should frequently be invited to share table. Sometimes it would be an expression of gratitude, perhaps for his having healed someone, or an indication of respect; sometimes it would be an occasion for him to teach. In that culture to share table was a very significant gesture. It was above all an expression of social inclusion.

On this occasion Jesus responds to the criticism levelled against him by recounting three parables.[8] There are two short parables presented in parallel and carefully matched in content and language: the parables of the lost sheep and the lost coin.[9] Then there is the longer and very familiar parable of the two lost sons, normally and misleadingly referred to as the parable of the prodigal son. In fact, I think that the usual emphasis on lostness in these parables is misplaced. In the Lukan context I prefer to see them as parables of seeking and finding that which is lost, a seeking which is demanding and costly, and a finding which calls for joyful celebration.[10] Matthew has a version of the first of these parables; the other two are found only in Luke. Each evangelist is responsible for the choice of context in which he places the parables, and for the particular interpretation or application he suggests at the end. The context chosen here by Luke probably reflects the original setting,[11] and in considering these parables it is important to keep the context in mind: Jesus is in the company of sinners, and the Pharisees show contempt for him ("this fellow") and manifest indifference and a lack of compassion for those with whom he dines. It is particularly to these that the parables are directed. For the purpose of this book I will omit the parables of the lost sheep and the lost coin, and focus on the parable of the two lost sons, one in a far, foreign pigsty, the other at home on the farm.[12]

The Lost Sons (15:11–32)

This is "one of the most touching and exquisite short stories in the pages of world literature."[13] I would think that the younger son would be in his late teens; the older would probably be counted as a young man, too, in our society.[14] The familiar text reads as follows:

> Then Jesus said, 'There was a man who had two sons. The younger of them said to his father, "Father, give me the share of the property that will belong to me." So he divided his property between them. A few days later the younger son gathered all he had and travelled to a distant country, and there he squandered his property in dissolute living. When he had spent everything, a severe famine took place throughout that country, and he began to be in need. So he went and hired himself out to one of the citizens of that country, who sent him to his fields to feed the pigs. He would gladly have filled himself with the pods that the pigs were eating; and no one gave him anything. But when he came to himself he said, "How many of my father's hired hands have bread enough and to spare, but here I am dying of hunger! I will get up and go to my father, and I will say to him, 'Father, I have sinned against heaven and before you; I am no longer worthy to be called your son; treat me like one of your hired hands.'" So he set off and went to his father. But while he was still far off, his father saw him and was filled with compassion; he ran and put his arms around him and kissed him. Then the son said to him, "Father, I have sinned against heaven and before you; I am no longer worthy to be called your son." But the father said to his slaves, "Quickly, bring out a robe—the best one—and put it on him; put a ring on his finger and sandals on his feet. And get the fatted calf and kill it, and let us eat and celebrate; for this son of mine was dead and is alive again; he was lost and is found!" And they began to celebrate.
>
> 'Now his elder son was in the field; and when he came and approached the house, he heard music and dancing. He called one of the slaves and asked what was going on. He replied, "Your brother has come, and your father has killed the fatted calf, because he has got him back safe and sound." Then he became angry and refused to go in. His father came out and began to plead with him. But he answered his father, "Listen! For all these years I have been working like a slave for you, and I have never disobeyed your command; yet you have never given me even a young goat so that I might celebrate with my friends. But when this son of yours came back, who has devoured your property with prostitutes, you killed the fatted calf for him!" Then the father said to him, "Son, you are always with me, and all that is mine is yours. But we had to celebrate and rejoice, because this brother of yours was dead and has come to life; he was lost and has been found."' (15:11–32)

The parable divides naturally into three parts, each suggested by the text itself: the departure and fall of the younger son; his return and welcome by the father; the father and the older brother. The father is the main character; his actions shape the way the narrative unfolds and provide the crucial turning points. The dynamics of human relationships and family life provide the field of comparison for the parable.[15]

Departure of The Younger Son

The opening statement recalls other men who had two sons: Adam with Cain and Abel; Abraham with Isaac and Ishmael; Isaac with the twins Jacob and Esau; Jacob's son Joseph with Manasseh and Ephraim; David was the youngest son of seven. In these cases, there is some sibling rivalry, and it is the younger son who is favoured. So, this would be the expectation of those listening to Jesus' parable, but parables don't usually follow expectations![16]

The father in the story is probably a farmer or landowner, and quite well-off. His younger son approaches him and asks for a share of the family estate. The legal situation in Jesus' time was complex. Some maintain that a father could dispose of his property during his lifetime, despite the cautions against such a course of action found in the book of Sirach (33:19–23), but it was highly unusual. Others believe that any transfer of the ownership of property normally took place after the father's death, so it was out of the ordinary for a son to ask for it. It has been suggested that the son's request may be considered as tantamount to wishing his father dead.[17] In that world, it was the family rather than the individual that was the source of identity; family loyalty was crucial. Solidarity with the village community was another key factor. Central to family identity was relationship to land, which should always remain in the family.[18] The implications of the young man's request are therefore considerable. On the other hand, given that younger sons often emigrated because of the precarious nature of the Palestinian agrarian economy, "the request should not be considered as rebellion or a desire for unwarranted freedom. It was legitimate, even if inappropriate."[19] In granting the request, which is couched rather like a command, the father demonstrates enormous love for his boy, and perhaps a little prodigality in giving the younger son half the estate rather than the usual one third.[20] But his reputation would suffer; he would lose honour and status in the village community; this he disregards.[21]

The father then probably sold some of the property "in order to provide the inheritance in liquid assets."[22] Some think that the father probably did not at this stage hand over the rest of the property to the older son, but remained master of the house and owner of the remaining property.[23] Others take the opposite view, as the text suggests.[24] "If the father deeded the property to his sons during his lifetime, the sons would normally have the right of possession, but not the right of disposal, since the father retained the use and enjoyment of the property."[25] The younger son wastes no time in moving off. He leaves home and family, rejecting all that it stands for. He is prepared to sever his relationship with his father, showing no regard for his feelings or future well-being. Leaving his brother does not seem to pose a problem; it appears that they are not particularly close. The elder brother apparently makes no attempt to mediate, to reconcile, as might have been expected in that culture;[26] he may have been annoyed that he had received only half rather than the expected two thirds. The closely knit village community would have been surprised and shocked at what had happened.

The young man sets off for the diaspora. There he irresponsibly squanders his money on a life of pleasure, self-indulgence and extravagance.[27] In doing so he completely disposes of his capital, making it impossible for him to offer support to his father in his old age; he thus severs the relationship and dishonours the family. It is this which constitutes his sin.[28]

The situation changes dramatically with the onset of famine. Penniless and without friends, his freedom dream in tatters, he is obliged to hire himself out to a Gentile landowner, who sends him to tend the pigs.[29] As a Jew, he is thus totally alienated, the epitome of lostness.[30] But his main problem is that he is starving to death, unable to eat the carob pods supplied to the pigs. No one bothers about his need. His hunger galvanises him into action.[31] "He came to his senses." He makes a snap decision to return home, where his father's "hired men have all the food they want."[32] He is prepared to acknowledge that he has done wrong in God's sight and has offended his father,[33] and there are signs of regret and remorse, but this probably does not amount to repentance. As he envisages a brighter future, though aware that he has forfeited his right to sonship and has no claims on his father, his plan is to ask his father to take him on as a hired servant. This would enable him to maintain his independence and social respectability living in the village. And he could use his income to fulfil the financial responsibilities to his father which he had selfishly abandoned. He seems to wish to return on his own terms, to do things his way. Some think that maybe this is not repentance so much as strategic conniving.[34] But he seems to assume that his father will look on him with a level of favour. "The hope of reconciliation, not restoration, brings him home."[35]

Return and Welcome

The spotlight switches and focuses on the father, who probably misses his son and worries about him, as would any father, and is on hopeful lookout. The key word in the whole parable (or the key phrase in translation), is, I believe, the verb which describes the father's (extravagant)[36] response when he catches sight of the returning younger son in the distance: "But while he was still far off, his father saw him and was filled with compassion; he ran and put his arms around him and kissed him."

All that follows in the narrative springs from compassion. He is that kind of man. The delighted father runs to meet his son.[37] Normally an elder would not run; it was socially unacceptable.[38] But it also enables him to meet the young man outside the village boundary and protect him from the inevitable hostility of the villagers, who probably gathered quickly. A remarkable reconciliation takes place.[39] The father says nothing; there is no lecture or blame or criticism. The past is past. His actions express his profound paternal love, acceptance and welcome. He kisses him repeatedly in a firm embrace, a sign of forgiveness, a recognising that he is his son, and this is public, for all the villagers to see. None of them will cause him harassment now.

The son forgets the crippling hunger which prompted his decision to return. As he begins his rehearsed speech,[40] using the term "father", his father interrupts before he can announce his plan of maintaining his independence as a hired servant rather than a son. He comes to realise that what is at issue is a broken relationship, a relationship which he cannot heal. The possibility of that relationship being re-established, his being reinstated as son, can only come as a pure gift from his father. He perceives from his father's behaviour that such an offer is being made. The gift of the best robe, ring and shoes, which the servants are ordered to bring, are clear indications of this; they are symbols of belonging and freedom, "emblematic of the son's honourable restoration to the family he had snubbed and abandoned."[41] The father's compassionate love brings about a change within him, and he graciously accepts the gift freely and generously offered, beyond his wildest dreams.[42] The father sets in motion the arrangements for a great celebration to which the whole village community would be invited, so as to participate in their rejoicing and share in the restoration and reconciliation which has occurred; it would also mend fractured village relationships.[43] The father sums up his view of things: "for this son of mine was dead and is alive again; he was lost and is found!" To the lost and found language of the two shorter parables is added the appropriate image of death and resurrection. The son had cut himself off from the life of the family, his village community and his religion; he was as good as dead; now he is alive once more. The family and community celebrate.

The Father and The Older Brother

The other son returns from the fields which will be his when his father dies. He gets wind of the party, for there is music in the air. He plies one of the local children, or one of the servants, with questions. The youngster without guile, using kinship language,[44] informs him that his brother has returned home and that his father has killed the fatted calf to celebrate. The older brother's reaction is one of anger;[45] he refuses to participate in the celebratory meal which has been prepared. He remains outside, refusing to join in the meal and the fun, and unwilling to fulfil his role as master of ceremonies. This is a public insult to his father.[46] The father reacts by coming out of the house and pleading with him.[47] Until now, he probably had not realised that the older son was lost to him; now he comes out searching for him. This was culturally quite shocking.[48] The latter's response reveals the extent of his alienation and resentment. There is no respect, no affection; he does not address his father as "father". "Listen" he begins in an accusatory tone, and goes on to complain bitterly, betraying the attitude of a slave rather than a son.[49] He is resentful, self-righteous about his impeccable obedience, disparagingly critical of his father's other son, whom he accuses of wasting his money on "prostitutes", and refuses to acknowledge him as his brother. Obviously, he is quite incapable of understanding and entering into his father's joy.[50]

From the father there is no outburst of anger, no criticism or rebuke, no recall to duty. Rather, he reaches out graciously with love and compassion, searching to bridge the gulf between them: "My son,[51] you are with me always and all I have is yours." He affectionately acknowledges his permanent and valued presence in the home, reassures him that his rights and inheritance are still secure and protected, and finally reminds him that it really is right and necessary to celebrate.[52] He explains his joy in the terms used earlier—dead and alive, lost and found—but this time "your brother" replaces "my son".[53] It is an appeal for understanding, for brotherly reconciliation and acceptance, an appeal that he should join them, the family, and the whole community in fellowship and festivity. The parable ends at this point, with an invitation, a fervent plea; and we never learn the sequel.[54] We do not know whether the elder brother joined the celebration, whether he was reconciled with his brother, or whether he continued to live in alienation as a slave.[55] In this way we, the listeners/readers are forced to think about our own reaction or response to this short story as it applies to our lives and experience.

The parable responds magnificently to the initial context. The sinners are sharing the banquet found by the searching Jesus. The religious leaders stand critically aloof, refusing the invitation to accept the good news and join the party.[56] The table fellowship of Jesus is a celebration of seeking and finding. Jesus' critics can "find themselves within the story and thereby be persuaded to embrace his practice of hospitality, enacting the welcoming grace of God's dominion."[57] The story challenges them to change their attitude to "sinners" and their understanding of God.[58]

Taken together, the three parables reflect the way in which Jesus understands his ministry, what he is about, as he daily seeks the lost and the needy, but refuses to write off the righteous and religious elite. At the same time, these parables reveal a great deal about Jesus' understanding of God. Jesus operates in the way he does, shares table fellowship as he does, because he knows the compassionate heart of his Father, his all-inclusive, unconditional love, his unreserved acceptance and approval.[59] Table fellowship expresses it all.[60]

Reflections

The parable suggests to me several lines of reflection. First, there is the context of the parable, the symbolic gesture of table fellowship, which, I believe, contains the whole Gospel in a nutshell. Through sharing table with those considered sinners and outcasts, Jesus revealed his understanding of God and of the nature of his mission. We cannot, therefore, avoid asking who the "sinners" and outcasts are in our society and our Church today, the despised, the written off, the fringe members, the voiceless minorities. Many young people would see themselves in this category. As disciples on mission we are obliged to find ways of reaching out to them, ways of seeking and finding them, and enabling them to see the face of the God of Jesus and to experience God's closeness and love touching their lives. As individuals and as Church, we need to show vision, creativity and courage in fashioning ways of making present in our contemporary world the realities of which Jesus' table fellowship was a sign: unreserved acceptance, genuine respect, hospitality, forgiveness, friendship. Scripture poses disconcerting questions and offers an uncomfortable critique of our attitudes and responses and of some of our structures. We need to ask ourselves how accepting, inclusive and open we are—as individuals, as families and communities, as Church. We need also to acknowledge that searching for those who may have gone astray can be costly. Young people form a particular group which often sits on the margins of Church life.[61] Are we going to leave them there? The recent synod was aimed at addressing this problem.

The parable revolves around three actors: the prodigal son, the older brother and the compassionate father. We can identify with each of them. The younger son is wilful, self-centred and thoughtless in initially asking for his inheritance and then leaving his father and village community and doing his own thing. He seems to have sown his wild oats. Even his decision to return shows mixed motivation. In our own lives, though we may not have been quite so dramatic in turning away from our Father, we've probably at times made a bit of a mess of things and experienced the loss, hopelessness and confusion which our mistakes have engendered. On our return, we have known the Father's generous welcome and unstinting forgiveness, and have been able to celebrate.[62]

Perhaps the younger son is a member of our family, or an acquaintance, or someone in our school, parish, workplace, religious formation community. We have probably experienced this kind of individualism, opting out and thoughtless rejection. And we have had to cope with it. How, then, do we enable a return? We may have to go out and search, reaching out in kindness, smothering our pain. Sometimes we may need just to sit patiently and wait, leaving the door open, alert for signs of movement and change. In either case are we ready with a warm and generous welcome, with forgiveness, restoration, a celebration even?[63]

The older son is perhaps the one with whom religious people can more easily identify. He has kept the rules, done his duty, played it safe—and yet missed the point. He is self-centred too, critical, judgemental, joyless, self-righteous. In spite of his always being with the father, he doesn't really know his father's heart. The parable is unfinished, leaving us wondering whether he finally accepted the father's invitation to join the celebration, surrendering to his love, or did he remain sulking and disillusioned outside? Was he reconciled to his brother? I suspect we recognise some of his traits in our own hearts and lives. Is family or community reconciliation something we currently need to be involved in?

Finally, the father in the parable shows remarkable qualities which we might seek to make our own in our dealings with young people and also with adults. He is consistent and faithful, compassionate and kind, patient and generous, welcoming, forgiving and inclusive. He is a wonderful model for parents, educators, carers, pastors. In telling this story Jesus also reveals so much about his Father. He is a God who searches for both of his sons, a God of amazing patience, compassion and forgiveness. Is this the God we have come to know, love and serve? Is this the God whom we reveal to others, especially the young and those with whom we live and those we seek to serve? It is so important to create space and make time to meet the God of Jesus, who gives us freedom and responsibility for our lives, who loves us whether we are near or far away, whose love is all-inclusive and unconditional, and who longs to give us all that He is and all that He has: "All I have is yours." This is an amazing statement which invites much prayerful pondering; it opens the door on God's overspilling, utterly altruistic and infinitely abundant love for each of us. The big challenge for us is to find ways of revealing this God to the young people of today. There can be no better way than that of Jesus himself. Let him be our guide.

Endnotes

1   The previous chapter of Luke's Gospel ends with the exhortation by Jesus: "he that has ears to hear, let him hear." Green, *Luke*, 569, notes the links with chapters 14 and 16, concerned with meals and hospitality (see 14:13; 14:21; 16:20). He sees the basic theme of chapter 15 to be Jesus' defence of his ministry, and an "implicit and open-ended invitation to his interlocutors to join him in reflecting in their practices God's own attitude towards sinners."

2   Carroll, *Luke*, 309. Green, *Luke*, 570, notes that in Luke, the tax-collectors and "sinners" have been presented as open to repentance (3:10–14; 5:27–32; 5:29–32; 7:35–60). The Pharisees, when presented *in tandem* with the scribes, consistently have the role of Jesus' foes (5:17–6:11; 7:29–30). Denis McBride, *The Parables of Jesus* (Chawton: Redemptorist Publications, 1999), 123, refers to the outcasts and the outraged! Evans, *Luke*, 583, comments on Luke's fondness for "all", which leads to a blurred picture.

3   This is important for Luke: 5:1, 15; 6:17, 27, 47, 49; 7:29; 8:8–18; 9:35; 10:16, 24, 39; 11:28, 31.

4   The Pharisees were a fairly broad group with no particular membership requirements except a serious commitment to the Law and a concern to apply it to their daily lives. Within them was a group called *haberim*, like a guild of friends or associates, who were very strict and who pledged to keep the Law very precisely. They avoided the "people of the land". See Kenneth E. Bailey, *The Good Shepherd* (London: SPCK, 2015), 111–112; Reid, *Parables*, 181. They themselves, for fear of ritual defilement, had strict purity rules and food restrictions, and would eat only with their own.

5   The verb (*diegongyzon*) is stronger than 19:7 (Zacchaeus); it means "kept grumbling aloud". See John R. Donahue, *The Gospel in Parable* (Philadelphia: Fortress, 1998), 147; Carroll, *Luke*, 310.

6   5:30; 7:34.

7   Green, *Luke*, 571, notes that Jesus is rejecting the values and norms of the religious elite. They are the primary audience for the coming parables.

8   Jan Lambrecht, *Once More Astonished: The Parables of Jesus* (New York: Crossroad, 1981), 25, observes that because these parables are well known they may have lost their evocative power and be no longer able to make an impact. This challenges us to find a way of bringing the message to expression again.

9   Several key terms are repeated. Green, *Luke*, 573, notes the escalation: 1 out of 100; 1 out of 10; 1 of 2. Lambrecht, *Astonished*, 26, refers to them as "twin-similitudes". He suggests, p. 28, that they were told together on the same occasion, and were in 'Q'; Matthew chose to omit the second.

10   Though, as Donahue, *Gospel*, 147, points out, the word "lost" appears five times in seven verses. McBride, *Luke*, 200, speaks of the experience of loss, the movement of search and the joy of discovery. Lambrecht, *Astonished*, 27, divides each into three sections: search; actions after the finding; application. Green, *Luke*, 573, reminds us that the finale of each refers to sinners and heaven, and so the parables are fundamentally about God.

11   Donahue, *Gospel,* 148. In Matthew (18:12–14) the parable is directed to his disciples, not to the Pharisees and scribes; it is an illustration of the type of leadership they should embrace.

12   McBride, *Parables,* 133, says "lost in the wilderness of his own self-righteous hostility."

13   McBride, *Luke,* 203.

14   Marshall, *Luke,* 607, suggests that the younger son would be unmarried and about eighteen years old.

15   Donahue, *Gospel,* 152–153; Carroll, *Luke,* 315; Francis J. Moloney, *Reflections on Evangelical Consecration* (Bolton: Don Bosco Publications, 2015), 79. Marshall, *Luke,* 604, takes the father as the central figure. Green, *Luke,* 578, however, maintains that the younger son occupies centre stage, and there are two responses to his recovery, compassion by the father and anger by the older brother. Lambrecht, *Astonished,* 31, suggests two sections, one dealing with the younger and the other with the older brother; both end in the same way (vv. 24 and 32: "lost and found"). The first part is similar to the two previous parables. On p. 46, he notes that the hearer is invited to enter into the drama of the (strange) family and approve the loving response of the father. He needs to decode its symbolic meaning and is then confronted with a choice. McBride, *Parables,* 134, speaks of a mixed human family in which tenderness, selfishness and hostility all vie with each other for possession.

16   Amy-Jill Levine, *Short Stories by Jesus* (New York: HarperOne, 2014), 50–51; Donahue, *Gospel,* 159; McBride, *Parables,* 137. Reid, *Parables,* 58, notes that in the Genesis stories women play a significant role; in this story there is no mention of a mother or daughter.

17   Reid, *Parables,* 59; Bailey, *Shepherd,* 161–169; McBride, *Parables,* 136. Carroll, *Luke,* 315, comments: "even if in effect it means that the son is treating him as if he were already dead." Donahue, *Gospel,* 154 says: "he acts as if his father were dead" in squandering the inheritance. Green, *Luke,* 580, comments that the son's request is presumptuous and highly irregular; "read as the first of a series of actions that lead to his characterisation as 'dead and lost', his request clearly signifies his rejection of his family." In n. 230, he suggests that Bailey seems to have overstated the case. Levine, *Stories,* 51, maintains that there is no Jewish support for the view of such as Bailey. On p. 313, n. 33, she suggests that Bailey bases himself on medieval Arab Christian interpretation and contemporary Arab custom.

18   Reid, *Parables,* 59; McBride, *Parables,* 134–35. He reminds us that in the ancient Mediterranean world, the family, not the individual, was the primary unit of importance and the psychological centre of life. Identity was family identity; individualism was shunned. Solidarity with the village came next in importance. "In the tightly-knit community of the village, where you lived your life in close proximity to relations and neighbours, social conformity was a matter of survival." One's identity was largely determined by whether you commanded their respect or not. Non-conformity was a threat to cohesion. On p. 135 he notes that central to family identity was its relationship to land. "The father's house" (the extended family) was the basic kinship structure, providing a sense of inclusion, identity and responsibility. The basic rule (tenaciously adhered to) was that land should remain

in the family (Lev 25:25). The Old Testament gives no example of an Israelite voluntarily selling land outside his family. It would be an economic tragedy and social disaster.

19   Donahue, *Gospel,* 153–54; Fitzmyer, *Luke,* 2:1087.

20   The Greek uses the word *bios,* as in Mark 12:44, regarding the widow. For Carroll, *Luke,* 315, this means his entire means of sustaining life.

21   Reid, *Parables,* 59; Tannehill, *Luke,* 240; McBride, *Parables,* 137: "In dividing his property among his two sons, he is flaunting traditional values and custom; other families in the village would probably close ranks against him lest they be affected by his shameless example."

22   Levine, *Stories,* 53. Others (like Marshall, *Luke,* 607) believe that the son made a further request to dispose of his share, a request which was granted. Reid, *Parables,* 60, suggests that he converted his inheritance into cash; Tannehill, *Luke,* 240, thinks that the son sells the land he has inherited.

23   Fitzmyer, *Luke,* 2:1087–1090.

24   Carroll, *Luke,* 315; on p. 318 he writes: "As the father observes, all the family's property belongs to his older son, though the father would retain his right to use it." Green, *Luke,* 580, says "the elder son receives his portion as well." Also, McBride, *Luke,* 206, adding that when the younger son leaves home he has no further claim on the home property, but he does have the obligation of supporting his father; similarly, Marshall, *Luke,* 607.

25   McBride, *Luke,* 206.

26   Reid, *Parables,* 59–60. Levine, *Stories,* 67, suggests that sibling rivalry is another biblical convention (Cain & Abel, Jacob & Esau, Leah & Rachel, Martha & Mary); and so, the relationship between the two was probably dysfunctional. McBride, *Parables,* 137, believes the elder brother is culpable of standing by while his family breaks up. He is now the sole owner of what remains of the estate, although the father retains the right to enjoy the produce.

27   Levine, *Stories,* 54. She suggests that he engages in gambling, alcohol abuse, sexual indulgence etc. She also thinks the father may be complicit in the son's debauchery by acquiescing to the son's request. However, it is the older brother who, only later, mentions inappropriate sexual activity.

28   Donahue, *Gospel,* 154. Green, *Luke,* 580, sees disposing of one's inheritance by turning it into transportable capital during the father's lifetime as a shocking breach of familial ties. Evans, *Luke,* 592, notes that it is the dissipation of the father's wealth which constitutes the wrong against him.

29   Levine, *Stories,* 56, observes that at the time of Jesus more Jews lived in Gentile territory than in the Jewish homeland, and they did relate to Gentiles. McBride, *Parables,* 138, sees him as a refugee and migrant worker; he depends on an "urbanite of some wealth".

30   Donahue, *Gospel,* 153, states that "he has lost his familial, ethnic and religious identity." Green, *Luke,* 581, notes that the practice of almsgiving was little

observed amongst the Greeks and Romans. Marshall, *Luke,* 608, refers to "the nadir of degradation".

31   This is the turning point (*krisis*) of the story. McBride, *Parables,* 139, suggests a chiastic structure.

32   The verb *anastas,* 'arise' or 'get up', "anticipates the motif of new life with which his father will interpret his return and restoration to the family" (Carroll, *Luke,* 316). Green, *Luke,* 582, sees the verb as beginning to signal his return to life from death. McBride, *Luke,* 205, sees the experience of failure and hopelessness as the pivotal point of the story. Moloney, *Reflections,* 80, sees the moment when the son recognises the depths to which his wastefulness has led him, as the turning point of the story. Reid, *Parables,* 60–61, sees no repentance here.

33   "Against heaven and against you" is a typical Old Testament expression; "heaven" is a circumlocution for God; the (empty) words are found in Pharaoh's mouth in Exod 10:16. Note the soliloquy.

34   Levine, *Stories,* 57–58, considers "coming to himself" as indicating that he knows that daddy will do what he asks: "I'll go to daddy and sound religious." Kenneth E. Bailey, *Poet and Peasant* and *Through Peasant Eyes* (Grand Rapids: Eerdmans, 1983), 173-180, refers to shrewdness and self-serving. Tannehill, *Luke,* 241, suggests that his return home may be motivated entirely by self-interest rather than any real feeling for the injury he has done to his father.

35   McBride, *Parables,* 139.

36   Carroll, *Luke,* 316, sees the father's reaction as "extravagant, prodigal, excessive." Reid, *Parables,* 61, as "most unexpected" of a patriarch grievously shamed.

37   Levine, *Stories,* 61–63, notes that Jewish fathers were not distant or wrathful; she quotes sayings and actions of Jesus in support (Matt 7:9; Jairus; the father of the boy with epilepsy). It would not be unnatural or surprising for a father to welcome back a wastrel son. "For the rabbis, the challenge is not in seeing God's love in a new way; the challenge—an inevitable challenge in any religious system—is to get the wayward to return."

38   Donahue, *Gospel,* 155; Green, *Luke,* 583; McBride, *Luke,* 207.

39   Carroll, *Luke,* 316, recalls Esau and Jacob (Gen 33:4). Marshall, *Luke,* 610, notes that the father's action is a sign of forgiveness and of the restoration of the broken relationship; the initiative is the father's.

40   Green, *Luke,* 582, notes that although the son acknowledges his sin and shame, it is his return which makes reconciliation possible. "The father's response, based solely on the return of his son, already undercuts the son's plans."

41   Green, *Luke,* 583. In n. 245, he notes that he is not being invested with his father's authority, as some suggest; the ring is not a signet ring; he probably needs clothing appropriate to his status in the family; they signify the restoration of his honour as a son. Lambrecht, *Astonished,* 32, believes that the forgiveness and restoration imply astonishingly more than the mere pardoning of offences. McBride, *Parables,* 142, recalls Gen 41:42. "The son is publicly restored to his position

within the hierarchy of the household." Marshall, *Luke,* 610, sees ring and shoes as symbols of authority and freedom; Reid, *Parables,* 61, as symbols of "distinction and authority".

42 Levine, *Stories,* 66, believes this view is "generous"; she prefers to see the favourite son as pampered and manipulative.

43 The slaughtering of an animal is a mark of the father's joy. Meat was not eaten often. With the reference to making merry, the first part of the parable ends (as did the two earlier ones). There is a double climax (Lambrecht, *Astonished,* 32). He refers to "end stress", more emphasis placed on what comes last. The first part of the parable prepares for the second. McBride, *Parables,* 143, sees the invitation of the villagers to the celebration as also restoring village relationships. Reid, *Parables,* 62, considers the meal to be a gesture of reconciliation with the members of the village, and their acceptance of the invitation a sign of reintegration into the community.

44 Carroll, *Luke,* 317, uses this term.

45 Green, *Luke,* 584, stresses the contrast in affective states: compassion and anger; they give rise to contrasting behaviours. On p. 585, n. 252, he notes that his wish to celebrate with friends rather than family breaches the kinship values operative in his world; also, McBride, *Parables,* 145. McBride, *Luke,* 208, sees him now as the "separated one", far from home.

46 McBride, *Parables,* 144, notes that the elder brother's absence makes family rivalry a public issue; his absence will be interpreted as a reproach to the villagers who are attending the feast.

47 The verb (*parakaleō*) can also mean to comfort.

48 Donahue, *Gospel,* 156. Reid, *Parables,* 63, notes that in a patriarchal world a father rules over his sons and never entreats them to do what is obligatory. Tannehill, *Luke,* 243, states that the father ignores his own dignity and position.

49 Levine, *Stories,* 72, observes that the elder son's comment would not have rung true to one of the real slaves in the household. Green, *Luke,* 585, notes that the elder son has apparently lived in alienation from his father. Lambrecht, *Astonished,* 31, considers the language unusually harsh. McBride, *Parables,* 144–145, notes that his self-image is that of being a slave.

50 Carroll, *Luke,* 318, comments that self-interest and the integrity of the family inheritance, not to mention the favouritism apparently being shown to the younger son, provoke the older son's protest. McBride, *Parables,* 145, notes how he believes he has not received due recognition; has been overlooked.

51 The Greek is *teknon,* child, conveying tenderness ("my dear son"). Levine, *Stories,* 73, observes that the father does not speak to the younger son; he communicates his love through his gestures. He expresses his love for the elder son in words, words which express their ongoing relationship.

52 The verb *dei* is used; Luke often uses this as indicating divine necessity.

53 Lambrecht, *Astonished,* 31, notes that the father repudiates the older brother's "this son of yours"; they are still brothers.

54   Moloney, *Reflections*, 81, suggests that the reason for this is that the main concern of Jesus is his presentation of the father.

55   Donahue, *Gospel*, 162. He stresses that the story does not convey a "patriarchal" father, concerned with authority and power. Quoting S. Schneiders: "God is the one who respects our freedom, mourns our alienation, waits patiently for our return, and accepts our love as pure gift" (*Women and the Word*, 1986). Green, *Luke*, 579, writes: "Against the interpretive horizons of the Roman world, wherein the characteristic attributes of the father as the *paterfamilias* are remembered especially in terms of authoritarianism and legal control, the picture Luke paints is remarkable for its counter-emphasis on care and compassion." Moloney, *Reflections*, 80, stresses the surprising attitude of the father who does not wish to dominate or possess, but gives them their freedom.

56   McBride, *Parables*, 146, notes that "the drama of the parable mirrors both Jesus' pastoral strategy towards sinners and the Pharisees' strategy of separation." There is an appeal to treat sinners with kindness, to move from a stance of separation to association.

57   Carroll, *Luke*, 313.

58   McBride, *Luke*, 204, writes: "Reaching out is more God-like than keeping away; association is more God-like than segregation." Lambrecht, *Astonished*, 33, suggests that the description of the indignant elder brother is given for the benefit of the Pharisees and fits them perfectly; they are invited to share the joy.

59   See P. Tournier, *Guilt and Grace* (London: Hodder & Stoughton, 1962), 189. Moloney, *Reflections*, 82, notes that the parable questions the way God was understood and revered in the religion and culture of his time.

60   Moloney, *Reflections*, 79, sees this parable as a paradigm of the role of God and subsequently of his Son, Jesus, in shepherding. On p. 81, he states that Jesus lived the parable he told. Marshall, *Luke*, 604, states that Jesus defends himself and his attitude to sinners by appeal to the attitude of God.

61   *Christus Vivit*, 39–42.

62   Pope Francis, in *Christus Vivit*, 2, writes: "However far you may wander, he is always there, the Risen One. He calls you and he waits for you to return to him and start over again." See also his reflection in 12.

63   Levine, *Stories*, 73–76. Reid, *Parables*, 64, notes the absence of a mother in the story, or a daughter. She maintains that female images are required which express equally well what the father image says of God. The second parable of the trio in which the woman householder is the protagonist, redresses this imbalance to some extent.

Conclusion

When embarking on the project of reflecting on the theme of 'Jesus and Young People', I did not expect to find the Gospel material quite so enriching and inspiring as it is. All the episodes in this book I had already studied, pondered, taught, and most of them already written about. But approaching them from a different angle, with a fresh focus on the young people involved, opened new avenues for reflection and has been really exciting. Usually we read and pray the stories or parables, as discrete items, which is the way they appear in the liturgical readings, but when considered together, the cumulative effect proves to be very powerful.

The Jesus we meet here is not new to us. He is, as we know, a man of great care and compassion, and this is borne out in almost every episode. In several of the stories he shows a strong desire to help, heal and bring life to the young, and is prepared to cross traditional barriers, cultural and religious, in order to reach them and respond to their needs. Two of the young people, the centurion's son and the Syro-Phoenician woman's daughter, are Gentiles; that does not prove to be an insurmountable obstacle for Jesus. Two other young people, the daughter of Jairus and the son of the widow of Nain, are dead, and Jesus ignores the implications of ritual defilement involved in being in contact with them so as to restore them to life and to the family. Neither the ridicule of mourners nor the disapproval of his disciples is able to deter him from making transforming contact with the young. Nor is he too proud to turn to a young boy in his need for bread and fish. There is a great inner freedom about Jesus; he is sensitive, generous, faithful and forgiving. The picture on the front cover of this book captures, I feel, his warmth and genuine concern, his joy in youthful company, his desire that they should be fully alive.

Whilst our attention is centred on the young people in the various episodes, we cannot but be struck by the love and care of the parents involved, and be moved by the pain and hope in their lives: Jairus, the Syro-Phoenician woman, the father of the boy suffering from a form of epilepsy, the mothers with their young children. These youngsters are so fortunate in having such devoted parents who are prepared to go to great lengths in their efforts to secure a cure or a blessing for their children. For a child to know that he/she is accepted and loved is so important. That experience is also a window into the mystery of God's love for them. But, sadly, this is not the case for all young people; and this is a great tragedy which can have lasting, negative consequences. As disciples of Jesus, we are called to find ways of redressing these situations. That is precisely what Don Bosco and others like him have sought to do over the years with great courage, compassion and creativity.

In his actions and his parables, Jesus comes across as someone very much in touch with the reality of his local world and culture, facing real situations, problems and experiences. Reflecting on the various episodes and the words of Jesus introduces us to such a wide spectrum of issues. A recurring factor is the need for faith and trust in him and in the Father, and the need to request God's help in prayer. Many of the qualities found in children are highlighted, like generosity, openness, keen perception, wonder, spontaneous expressions of joy; and many needs are exposed: the need to be listened to and taken seriously, guided and supported, accepted and encouraged. As adults, we are challenged to cross barriers, to abandon our fears and prejudices, to touch, to be aware, to get involved, to reach out not only to the young, but to the elderly, needy and vulnerable in our society as well. We have been reminded of the problems posed for young people by our secularised society, and of our need to offer alternative values through our own way of thinking and living. The issue of requests and responses, positive and negative, such a feature of our lives, has been raised, and we have been spurred on to recall the times when we have been let down or have let others down, or think of no-win situations in which we have been involved.

Of the many issues raised by these encounters and by the parables of Jesus, two stand out for me. The first is the aspect of receptivity highlighted in Jesus' blessing the young people brought to him. In stressing the vulnerability and basic neediness of children, their dependence on adults, Jesus is reminding us not only about our need to care for them, but also that we need not seek to win God's love, we do not merit salvation; our efforts, position, skillset, qualities, status are irrelevant. Like children, we receive with open hands, receive with joy and gratitude the free gift of God made available through Jesus—our sharing in God's life as God's cherished sons and daughters. "All I have is yours", says the father in the parable of the two lost sons. The attitude of the centurion in Capernaum and the woman in the district of Tyre are relevant here. Both are aware that they have no right to Jesus' intervention, no automatic claims; they know that they are dependent on his generosity.[1] There is a wonderful poverty of spirit about them both. What they receive, what their children receive, comes as a free gift. This is true for us.

The second issue perhaps runs parallel to the first. Jesus' acts of healing, exorcising and raising to life, make it clear that he has authority and power. Yet, in his mind they are acts of love and service. Status, control, domination, superiority and so on were permanent and universal factors in the culture of Jesus' day, and his disciples were no exception to that mindset. Our culture today is no different. As adults we are inevitably in the stronger position relative to young people. We have to be realistic about that. However, Jesus emphasises our need to see ourselves as servants, willing to relinquish control at times, willing to listen and learn, open to change our attitudes and ways of doing things. The servant, self-giving style of Jesus must characterise our presence with the young, and the way we seek to respond to them and share their lives. If at times we are obliged to challenge or make demands, it should clearly spring from love, from the desire for their growth, wholeness and well-being. One important aspect of Jesus-like service is the ability to forgive. We all fail and make mistakes, the disciples of Jesus did so in spectacular fashion, but Jesus is faithful to them, sticks with them, forgives, and offers a fresh start.

I deliberately chose as my final chapter the parable which illustrates so well the rationale for Jesus' way of living his ministry, his option for sharing table with those on the margins, his seeking the lost, his desire to share their lives and enable them to embrace God's kingly rule. In telling that wonderful story, Jesus was sharing his understanding of the Father's heart, the Father's compassion, goodness, generosity and forgiveness, the Father's "all-inclusive, unconditional love, his unreserved acceptance and approval."[2] Through Jesus and his Spirit-gift, we are invited to come to know that Father more closely. It is the Father's love which we seek to reflect in our dealings with the young. It is the way of Jesus which we seek to imitate. May our prayerful reflection on these Gospel texts strengthen us in our resolve to do so.

Endnotes

1. Eph 2:2–10 puts this very beautifully.
2. Tournier, *Guilt and Grace,* 189.

Bibliography

Mark

Anderson, Hugh. *The Gospel of Mark*. London: Oliphants, 1976.

Boring, M. Eugene. *Mark. A Commentary.* NTL Louisville & London: Westminster John Knox, 2006.

Byrne, Brendan. *A Costly Freedom*. Collegeville, MN: Liturgical Press, 2008.

Cranfield, Charles E. B. *The Gospel according to St. Mark*. Cambridge: Cambridge University Press, 1959.

Culpepper, R. Alan. *Mark*. Macon: Smyth and Helwys, 2007.

Donahue, John R. and Harrington, Daniel H. *The Gospel of Mark*. Sacra Pagina 2. Collegeville, MN: Liturgical Press, 2002.

Harrington, Wilfrid. *Mark*. Dublin: Veritas, 1979.

Hooker, Morna D. *The Message of Mark*. London: Epworth Press, 1983; *The Gospel according to St. Mark*. London: A&C Black, 1991.

Kingsbury, Jack D. *The Christology of Mark's Gospel*. Philadelphia: Fortress Press, 1983.

McBride, Denis. *The Gospel of Mark*. Dublin: Dominican Publications, 1996.

Malbon, Elizabeth S. *In the Company of Jesus: Characters in Mark's Gospel*. Louisville: Westminster John Knox, 2000.

_____. *Mark's Jesus. Characterisation as Narrative Christology*. (Wac: Baylor University Press, 2009.

Martin, George. *The Gospel according to Mark*. Chicago: Loyola, 2005.
Moloney, Francis J. *The Gospel of Mark. A Commentary*. Peabody, MA: Hendrickson, 2002.
_____. *Mark, Storyteller, Interpreter, Evangelist*. Peabody, MA: Hendrickson, 2004.
_____. *Gospel Interpretation and Christian Life*. Adelaide: ATF Press, 2017.
Nineham, Dennis E. *St. Mark*. London: Penguin Books, 1963.
Rhoads, David. Dewey, Joanna. Michie, Donald. *Mark as* Story. Minneapolis: Fortress, 1999.
Senior, Donald. *The Passion of Jesus in the Gospel of Mark*. Wilmington, DE: Glazier, 1984.
Schweizer, Eduard. *The Good News according to Mark*. London: SPCK, 1971.
Shiner, Whitney. *Proclaiming the Gospel: First Century Performance of Mark*. London: Continuum, 2003.
Wright N. Tom. *Mark for Everyone*. London: SPCK, 2001.

Matthew

Beare, Francis W. *The Gospel according to Matthew*. Oxford: Blackwell, 1981.
Byrne, Brendan. *Lifting the Burden*. Collegeville, MN: Liturgical Press, 2004.
Davies, William D. and Allison, Dale C. *A Critical and Exegetical Commentary on the Gospel according to Saint Matthew*. London: T&T Clark, 2004.
Green, H. Benedict. *The Gospel according to Matthew*. London: Oxford University Press, 1975.
Gundry, Robert H. *Matthew*. Grand Rapids, MI: Eerdmans, 1994.
Hagner, Donald A. *Matthew*. Word Biblical Commentary. 2 vols. Nashville: Nelson, 2000.
Harrington, Daniel. *The Gospel of Matthew*. Sacra Pagina 1. Collegeville, MN: Liturgical Press, 1991.
Hill, David. *The Gospel of Matthew*. London: Oliphants, 1972.
Luz, Ulrich. *Matthew*. 3 vols. Minneapolis, MN: Augsburg Fortress, 2001, 2005, 2007.
Meier, John P. *Matthew*. Dublin: Veritas, 1980.
Senior, Donald. *Matthew*. Nashville: Abingdon Press, 1998.
Schweizer, Eduard. *The Good News according to Matthew*. London: SPCK, 1975.

Wright, N. Tom. *Matthew for Everyone*. 2 vols. London: SPCK, 2002.

Luke

Byrne, Brendan. *The Hospitality of God*. Collegeville, MN: Liturgical Press, 2000.
Caird, George B. *St. Luke*. London: Pelican, 1963.
Carroll, John T. *Luke: A Commentary*. Louisville: Westminster John Knox Press, 2012.
Evans, Christopher F. *Saint Luke*. London: SCM, 1990.
Fitzmyer, Joseph A. *The Gospel according to Luke*. 2 vols. New York: Doubleday, 1981, 1985.
Green, Joel B. *The Gospel of Luke*, NICNT. Cambridge: Eerdmans, 1997.
Johnson, Luke T. *The Gospel of Luke*, Sacra Pagina 3. Collegeville, MN: Liturgical Press, 1991.
Karris, Robert J. *Luke: Artist and Theologian*. New York: Paulist Press, 1985.
LaVerdiere, Eugene. *Luke*. Dublin: Veritas, 1980.
Marshall, I. Howard. *The Gospel of Luke*. Exeter: Paternoster Press, 1978.
Moloney, Francis J. *This is the Gospel of the Lord (C)*. Homebush: St Paul Publications, 1991.
McBride, Denis. *The Gospel of Luke*. Dublin: Dominican Publications, 1991.
Rasseguie, James L. *Spiritual Landscape*. Peabody MA: Hendrikson, 2004
Tannehill, Robert C. *Luke*. Nashville: Abingdon Press, 1996.
Thompson, G.H.P. *The Gospel according to Luke*. Oxford: Clarendon Press, 1972.
Winstanley, Michael T. *Walking with Luke*. Bolton: Don Bosco Publications, 2017.
Wright, N. Tom. *Luke for Everyone*. London: SPCK, 2001.

John

Barrett, C. Kingsley. *The Gospel according to John*, 2nd ed. London: SPCK, 1978.
Brown, Raymond E. *The Gospel according to John*, 2 vols. London: Chapmans, 1972.
Byrne, Brendan. *Life Abounding*. Strathfield NSW: St Pauls Publications, 2014.
Carter W., *John*. Peabody, MA: Hendrickson, 2006.
Chennattu, Rekha M. *Johannine Discipleship as a Covenant Relationship*. Peabody MA: Hendrickson, 2006.
Coloe Mary L. *God Dwells with Us*. Collegeville, MN: Liturgical Press, 2001.

Coloe Mary L. *Dwelling in the Household of God.* Collegeville, MN: Liturgical Press, 2007.

Culpepper, R. Alan. *Anatomy of the Fourth Gospel.* Philadelphia: Fortress Press, 1983.

_____. *The Gospel and Letters of John.* Nashville: Abingdon, 1998.

Dodd, Charles H. *The Interpretation of the Fourth Gospel.* Cambridge: CUP, 1968.

Koester, Craig R. *Symbolism in the Fourth Gospel.* Minneapolis: Fortress Press, 2003

_____. *The Word of Life.* Grand Rapids, MI: Eerdmans, 2008.

Lee, Dorothy A. *The Symbolic Narratives of the Fourth Gospel.* Sheffield: JSOT, 1994

_____. *Flesh and Glory.* New York: Crossroad, 2002.

_____. 'Friendship, Love and Abiding in the Gospel of John', in Rekha M. Chennattu and Mary L. Coloe, eds. *Transcending Boundaries. Contemporary Readings of the New Testament. Essays in Honour of Francis J. Moloney.* Rome: LAS, 2005.

Lincoln, Andrew T. *The Gospel according to Saint John.* Grand Rapids, MI: Baker Academic, 2005.

Lindars, Barnabas. *The Gospel of John.* London: Oliphants, 1972.

Moloney, Francis J. *The Gospel of John.* Sacra Pagina 4. Collegeville, MN: Glazier, 1998.

Schnackenburg, Rudolf. *The Gospel according to St. John,* 3 vols. London: Burns & Oates, 1968, 1980, 1982.

Senior, Donald. *The Passion of Jesus in the Gospel of John.* Leominster: Gracewing, 1991.

Schneiders, Sandra M. *Written That You May Believe.* New York: Crossroad, 1999.

_____. *Jesus Risen in our Midst.* Collegeville, MN: Liturgical Press, 2013.

_____. 'The Resurrection (of the Body) in the Fourth Gospel: A Key to Johannine Spirituality', in Donahue John R. ed. *Life in Abundance. Studies of John's Gospel in Tribute to Raymond E. Brown.* Collegeville, MN, Liturgical Press, 2005.

Winstanley, Michael T. *Symbols and Spirituality.* Bolton: Don Bosco Publications, 2007.

Yee, G.A. *Jewish Feasts and the Gospel of John.* Collegeville, MN: Liturgical Press, 1989.

Zevini, Giorgio. *Vangelo secondo Giovanni,* 2 vols. Rome: Città Nuova, 1998.

Other Books

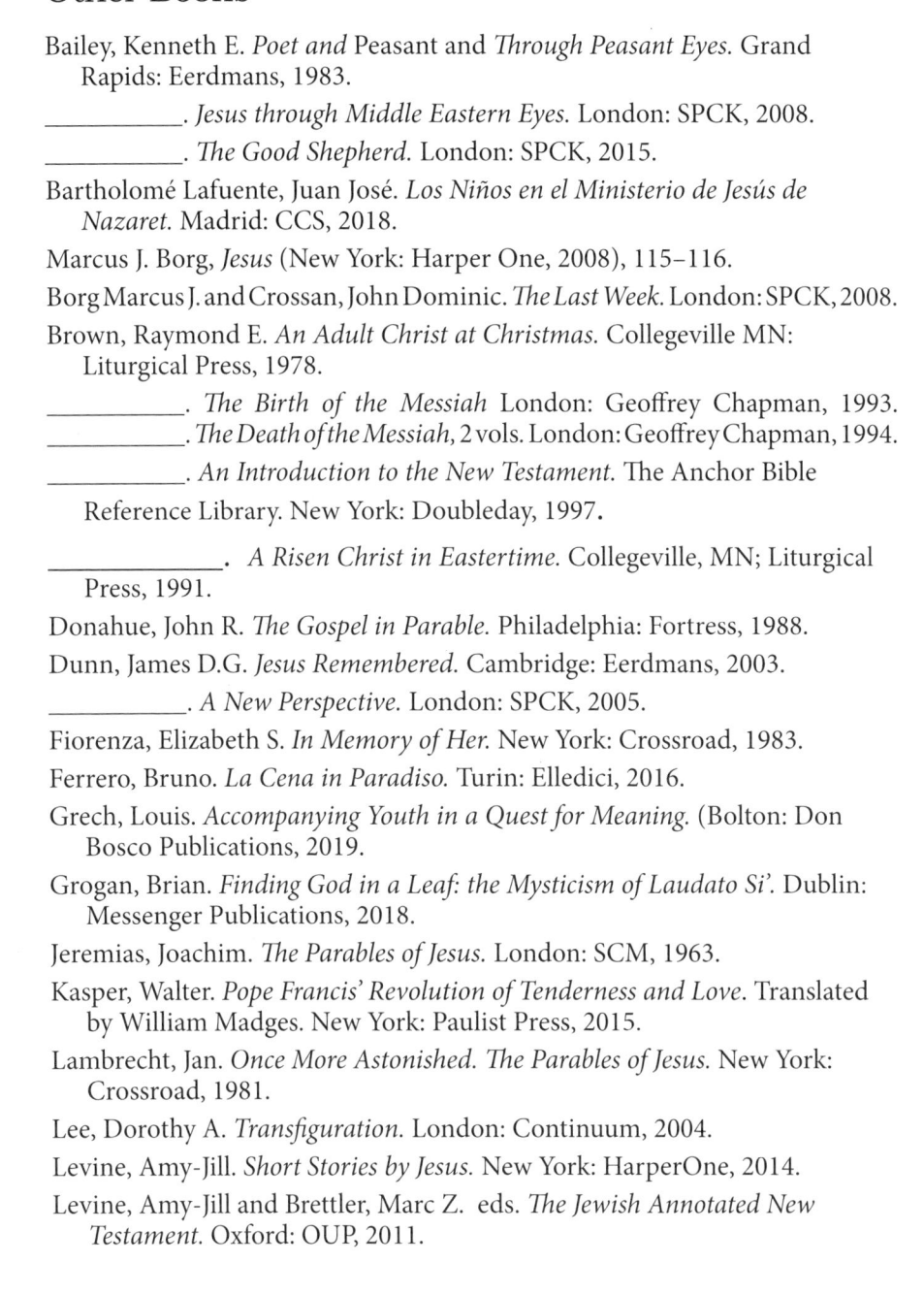

Bailey, Kenneth E. *Poet and* Peasant and *Through Peasant Eyes*. Grand Rapids: Eerdmans, 1983.

_____. *Jesus through Middle Eastern Eyes*. London: SPCK, 2008.

_____. *The Good Shepherd*. London: SPCK, 2015.

Bartholomé Lafuente, Juan José. *Los Niños en el Ministerio de Jesús de Nazaret*. Madrid: CCS, 2018.

Marcus J. Borg, *Jesus* (New York: Harper One, 2008), 115–116.

Borg Marcus J. and Crossan, John Dominic. *The Last Week*. London: SPCK, 2008.

Brown, Raymond E. *An Adult Christ at Christmas*. Collegeville MN: Liturgical Press, 1978.

_____. *The Birth of the Messiah* London: Geoffrey Chapman, 1993.

_____. *The Death of the Messiah*, 2 vols. London: Geoffrey Chapman, 1994.

_____. *An Introduction to the New Testament*. The Anchor Bible Reference Library. New York: Doubleday, 1997.

_____. *A Risen Christ in Eastertime*. Collegeville, MN; Liturgical Press, 1991.

Donahue, John R. *The Gospel in Parable*. Philadelphia: Fortress, 1988.

Dunn, James D.G. *Jesus Remembered*. Cambridge: Eerdmans, 2003.

_____. *A New Perspective*. London: SPCK, 2005.

Fiorenza, Elizabeth S. *In Memory of Her*. New York: Crossroad, 1983.

Ferrero, Bruno. *La Cena in Paradiso*. Turin: Elledici, 2016.

Grech, Louis. *Accompanying Youth in a Quest for Meaning*. (Bolton: Don Bosco Publications, 2019.

Grogan, Brian. *Finding God in a Leaf: the Mysticism of Laudato Si'*. Dublin: Messenger Publications, 2018.

Jeremias, Joachim. *The Parables of Jesus*. London: SCM, 1963.

Kasper, Walter. *Pope Francis' Revolution of Tenderness and Love*. Translated by William Madges. New York: Paulist Press, 2015.

Lambrecht, Jan. *Once More Astonished. The Parables of Jesus*. New York: Crossroad, 1981.

Lee, Dorothy A. *Transfiguration*. London: Continuum, 2004.

Levine, Amy-Jill. *Short Stories by Jesus*. New York: HarperOne, 2014.

Levine, Amy-Jill and Brettler, Marc Z. eds. *The Jewish Annotated New Testament*. Oxford: OUP, 2011.

Lohfink, Gerhard. *Jesus of Nazareth. What He wanted. Who He was.* Translated by Linda M. Maloney. Collegeville, MN: Liturgical Press, 2012.

_____. *Is This All There Is? On Resurrection and Eternal Life.* Translated by Linda M. Maloney. Collegeville, MN: Liturgical Press, 2017.

Martin, James. *Jesus, a Pilgrimage.* New York: HarperCollins, 2014.

McBride, Denis. *The Parables of Jesus.* Chawton: Redemptorist Publications, 1999.

McIver, Robert K. *Memory, Jesus and the Synoptic Gospels.* Atlanta: Society of Biblical Literature, 2011.

Meier, John P. *A Marginal Jew,* vol 2. London: Doubleday, 1994.

Metzger, B. M. *A Textual Commentary on the Greek New Testament.* London: United Bible Societies, 1971.

Moloney, Francis J. *The Resurrection of the Messiah.* New York: Paulist Press, 2013.

_____. *Living Voice of the Gospel.* Dublin: Veritas, 2006.

_____. *A Body Broken for a Broken People. Marriage, Divorce, and the Eucharist.* Mulgrave: Garratt, 2015.

_____. *Reading the New Testament in the Church. A Primer for Pastors, Religious Educators, and Believers.* Grand Rapids, MI: Baker Academic, 2015.

_____. *Reflections on Evangelical Consecration.* Bolton: Don Bosco Publications, 2015.

Pagola, José A. *Jesus, An Historical Approximation.* Miami: Convivium, 2011.

Perrin, Nicholas. *Jesus the Temple.* London: SPCK, 2010.

Pope Francis, *Laudato si': On Care for our Common Home* (London: St Pauls Publishing, 2015).

_____. *Christus Vivit* (Christ is Alive). London: CTS, 2019.

Reid, Barbara E. *Parables for Preachers (Year C).* Collegeville, MN: Liturgical Press, 2000;

Sala, Rosanno. *A Guidebook for Salesian Young People and Those who Work with Them.* Bolton: Don Bosco Publications, 2020.

Schneiders, Sandra M. 'Religious Life as Prophetic Life Form', in T*he National Catholic Reporter,* Jan 4–8, 2010.

_____. *Jesus Risen in our Midst.* Collegeville, MN: Liturgical Press, 2013.

Tournier, Paul. *Guilt and Grace.* London: Hodder & Stoughton, 1962.

Voorwinde, Stephen. *Jesus' Emotions in the Gospels.* London: T&T Clark, 2011.

Winstanley, Michael T. *Come and See.* London: DLT, 1985.

_____. *Don Bosco's Gospel Way.* Bolton: Don Bosco Publications, 2002.

_____. *Lenten Sundays.* Bolton: Don Bosco Publications, 2011.

_____. *Jesus and the Little People.* Bolton: Don Bosco Publications, 2012.
_____. *An Advent Journey.* Bolton: Don Bosco Publications, 2014.
_____. *Walking with Luke.* Bolton: Don Bosco Publications, 2017.
_____. *Alive.* Bolton: Don Bosco Publications, 2018.
_____. *Salesian Gospel Spirituality.* Bolton: Don Bosco Publications, 2020.
Wright, N. Tom. *Jesus and the Victory of God.* London: SPCK, 2000.
_____. *The Challenge of Jesus.* London: SPCK, 2000.
_____. *The Resurrection of the Son of God.* London: SPCK, 2003.
_____. *Surprised by Scripture.* London: SPCK, 2014.
Young, Brad H. *Jesus the Jewish Theologian.* Peabody, MA: Hendrickson, 1995.
Zerwick, Max and Grosvenor Mary. *An Analysis of the Greek New Testament.* Rome: Biblical Institute Press, 1974.

About the Author

Michael T. Winstanley is a Salesian of Don Bosco. He is a graduate of the Salesian Pontifical University, Rome, and London University. He lectured in biblical studies at Ushaw College, Durham, for seventeen years. Michael has spent many years in Formation Ministry, served twice as Provincial of the British Province, given retreats in many countries and been involved in a variety of adult education programmes. For twelve years, he worked with the Salesian volunteers at Savio Retreat House in Bollington, and he was Vicar for Religious in the Salford Diocese for five years. This is his twelfth book.

Other Books by Michael T. Winstanley SDB

An Advent Journey. Bolton: Don Bosco Publications, 2014.

Alive! The Gospel Resurrection Narratives: Then and Now. Bolton: Don Bosco Publications, 2018.

Come and See. London: Darton, Longman and Todd, 1985.

Don Bosco's Gospel Way. Bolton: Don Bosco Publications, 2002.

Into Your Hands. Homebush, NSW: St Paul's Publications, 1994.

Jesus and the Little People. Bolton: Don Bosco Publications, 2012.

Lenten Sundays. Bolton: Don Bosco Publications, 2011.

Salesian Gospel Spirituality: An Exploration, Bolton: Don Bosco Publications, 2020.

Scripture, Sacraments, Sprituality. Essex: McCrimmon Publishing Co. Ltd., 2002.

Symbols and Spirituality. Bolton: Don Bosco Publications, 2007.

Walking with Luke: Thematic Studies in the Lukan Narative with Reflections Bolton: Don Bosco Publications, 2017.